QuickBooks

A Complete Guide to Bookkeeping and Accounting for Small Businesses for Beginners

Marcus Smalling

© Copyright 2019 - All rights reserved.

The content contained within this book may not be reproduced, duplicated or transmitted without direct written permission from the author or the publisher.

Under no circumstances will any blame or legal responsibility be held against the publisher, or author, for any damages, reparation, or monetary loss due to the information contained within this book. Either directly or indirectly.

Legal Notice:

This book is copyright protected. This book is only for personal use. You cannot amend, distribute, sell, use, quote or paraphrase any part, or the content within this book, without the consent of the author or publisher.

Disclaimer Notice:

Please note the information contained within this document is for educational and entertainment purposes only. All effort has been executed to present accurate, up to date, and reliable, complete information. No warranties of any kind are declared or implied. Readers acknowledge that the author is not engaging in the rendering of legal, financial, medical or professional advice. The content within this book has been derived from various sources. Please consult a licensed professional before attempting any techniques outlined in this book.

By reading this document, the reader agrees that under no circumstances is the author responsible for any losses, direct or indirect, which are incurred as a result of the use of information contained within this document, including, but not limited to, — errors, omissions, or inaccuracies.

Table of Contents

What is QuickBooks & How Do Businesses Use It? 12
What Small Businesses Use QuickBooks for? 12
    1.   Manage Sales and Income 13
    2.   Monitor Bills and Expenses 15
    3.   Increase Key Reporting Insights to Your Business 16
    4.   Run Payroll 19
    5.   Track Inventory 20
    6.   Improve Taxes 20
    7.   Accept Online Payments 21
    8.   Scan Receipts 21
    Among the manners in which I can assist you with QuickBooks include: . 28
Picking the right QuickBooks plan 29
QuickBooks Online 31
    Pricing 31
    Features 31
QuickBooks Pro 33
    Pricing 33
    Features 34
QuickBooks Premier 36
    Pricing 36
    Features 36
QuickBooks Enterprise 38
    Pricing 38
    Features 39
QuickBooks Self-Employed 40
    Pricing 41

Features 41

QuickBooks Online Self-Employed 43

QuickBooks Online Simple Start: 44

QuickBooks Online Essentials 44

QuickBooks Online Plus 44

QuickBooks Online Advanced 45

QuickBooks Desktop Pro, Pro Plus and Mac 45

QuickBooks Desktop Premier and Premier Plus 46

How to Choose the Right Version of QuickBooks for Your Business 48

    Do You Want Cloud-Based or Locally-Installed Software? 48

    Are You A Mac or Windows User? 50

    What number of Users Do You Need? 50

    The amount Accounting Experience Do You Have? 51

    1.   Find an accountant. 52

    2.   Review the QuickBooks basics. 53

    3.   Set up a secure environment. 53

    4.   Enter your business, vitals. 54

    5.   Enter client data. 55

    6.   Enter essential seller and representative data. 56

    7.   Start following the cash stream. 56

    8.   Review expense labels and confirm them with a bookkeeper. 57

    9.   Create your first profit and loss report. 58

    10.   Include features as required. 59

        Including your first customer 60

        Including an accountant user 61

    Our Conversion Tips… 61

    Thoughts on Wholesale Billing 62

A quick preview of next week... 63
Basic Steps to Operating QuickBooks 65
10.	Get certified (and watch your firm develop!) 85
QuickBooks Online Advanced Payroll - Getting started............................... 87
   Set up 89
   Enter your organization data... 90
   Enter your payroll tax details 91
   CRA Account number 91
   Remittance frequency.. 92
   Workers' compensation 93
   Include banking data.. 95
   Add payroll settings 98
   Add employees and contractors 101
Map your chart of accounts 102
   Updates: 105
Create, edit, and manage budgets 105
   Set the money related year's first month 106
   Review historical amounts 106
Create your budget... 12
Budget reports.. 109
How to Use QuickBooks Efficiently... 123
   Bonus.. 126
   1.	Incorporate Your Digital Order-Taking Solution with QuickBooks.. 127
   2.	Enter Multiple Items with the Same Name and Account Type All at Once 127
   3.	Save Time by Creating a Custom Report 128
   4.	Utilize Attachments... 128

5. Change Default Email Text Settings for Invoices, Pay Stubs, Statements 128

6. Set Up Bank Rules for Common Expenses 129

7. Customize Your QuickBooks Icon Bar 129

8. Invest Time to Learn QuickBooks Correctly 129

9. Be Consistent in How You Classify Your Expenses 130

10. Utilize the QuickBooks Audit Trail to Protect Against Risk 130

Would I be able to record my assessments with QuickBooks Self-Employed? 131

How does QuickBooks Self-Employed assistance me with my Quarterly Taxes? 131

How would I run my year-end reports? 131

Regular Deductions for the Independently Employed 137

Travel and hotel 137

Home office 137

Utilities 138

Professional development 138

Advertising and marketing 139

Website 139

Software 139

Mileage and gas 139

Incorporation 140

Self-employment health insurance deduction 140

Learn the basics about QuickBooks File Manager 142

What would you be able to do in QuickBooks File Manager? 143

How can it work? 143

Three different ways to begin QuickBooks File Manager 144

Two different ways to import QuickBooks records 144

Open the organization record from File Manager 145

Manage and Merge customer folders 145

    Password Vault 146

    Batch Upgrade (Does not apply to the UK) 146

    File Manager backup 147

Recommendations to Resolve Performance Issues 148

Move your Company Files to Another Computer 158

How to Set Up a New Sales Tax Code 163

Alter Sales Tax Rate in QuickBooks Online 165

Look at QuickBooks Sales Tax 167

How QuickBooks Sales Tax Works 169

Need to Learn QuickBooks for Free? 174

    1. QuickBooks Tutorials 175

    2. QuickBooks Learning Center 175

    3. QuickBooks-Training.net 175

    4. QuickBooks Training 176

    5. Fit Small Business 176

    6. GCF Learn Free 176

    7. QuickBooks Explained 177

    8. Udemy 177

    9. Dummies 178

    10. Better Bottom Line 178

    11. LinkedIn Learning 179

Ways QuickBooks Can Help Run Your Small Business 180

QuickBooks Tips to Simplify Your Life 187

Let's Be Clear About What QuickBooks Online Advanced is Not 196

QuickBooks Online Advanced isn't Available on Wholesale ... Yet 196

QuickBooks Online Advanced Will Continue to Evolve and isn't done yet . 197

You Can Shape QuickBooks Online Advanced 197

Help and Support: 197

Conclusion 200

What is QuickBooks & How Do Businesses Use It?

QuickBooks is a small business bookkeeping software program organization use to manage deals and costs and monitor everyday exchanges. You can utilize it to receipt clients, pay the bills, produce reports for arranging, charge recording, and that's just the beginning. The QuickBooks product offering incorporates a few arrangements that work incredible for anybody from a solopreneur to a fair-sized business.

Since there are a few QuickBooks arrangements, it's significant that you pick the correct one. Before you submit, take QuickBooks for a turn by pursuing a free 30-day trial; the trial is an instrumental version of QuickBooks so that you can test the entirety of the fancy bells and whistles. The best part is that no charge card is required.

What Small Businesses Use QuickBooks for?

Small Businesses typically use QuickBooks to deal with their invoices, cover their bills, and track their incomes. They also use it to produce month-and year-end budgetary reports just as get ready for quarterly or yearly business charges. It's normal for entrepreneurs to manage QuickBooks themselves or utilize an in-house or outsourced bookkeeper.

The best eight QuickBooks small business utilizes are:

1. Manage Sales and Income

You can manage deals and salary in QuickBooks by making invoices to follow deals by the client. Remain over what clients owe you (also called your records receivable balance) by evaluating your Accounts Receivable Aging Report, which incorporates the details of both present and past due invoices. The following is an example A/R Aging Report from QuickBooks.

Large organizations will take a look at QuickBooks Premier or QuickBooks Enterprise, contingent upon the number of clients they need.

How Many Users Do You Need?

The number of clients you need will also help figure out which software is best for your business. Investigate this graph to see which item suits your business' size.

QuickBooks Self-Employed:	1 user
QuickBooks Pro:	1 – 3 users
QuickBooks Premier:	1 – 5 users
QuickBooks Online:	1 – 25 users
QuickBooks Enterprise:	1 – 30 users

Note: This diagram shows the most extreme number of clients available with every version of QuickBooks, which may cost extra.

How Much Accounting Experience Do You Have?

If you don't think a lot about accounting, you'll need to avoid QuickBooks Pro, Premier, or Enterprise, except if you're willing to place in an opportunity to learn.

QuickBooks Online and QuickBooks Self-Employed are many simpler choices to get a handle if you don't have much understanding or need to continue adjusting the books.

Then again, in case you're an accountant or somebody with much accounting experience, you may like the difficulty of the QuickBooks work area choices as they stick to progressively conventional accounting practices.

Paul's Plumbing
A/R AGING SUMMARY
As of September 30, 2016

	CURRENT	1 - 30	31 - 60	61 - 90	91 AND OVER	TOTAL
Amy's Bird Sanctuary		239.00				$239.00
Bill's Windsurf Shop			85.00			$85.00
▼ Freeman Sporting Goods						$0.00
0969 Ocean View Road	477.50					$477.50
55 Twin Lane		4.00	81.00			$85.00
Total Freeman Sporting Goods	**477.50**	**4.00**	**81.00**			**$562.50**
Geeta Kalapatapu	629.10					$629.10
Jeff's Jalopies		81.00				$81.00
John Melton		450.00				$450.00
Kookies by Kathy		75.00				$75.00
Mark Cho	314.28					$314.28
Paulsen Medical Supplies	954.75					$954.75
Red Rock Diner	70.00			156.00		$226.00
Rondonuwu Fruit and Vegi	78.60					$78.60
▼ Shara Barnett						$0.00
Barnett Design		274.50				$274.50
Total Shara Barnett		**274.50**				**$274.50**
Sonnenschein Family Store	362.07					$362.07
Sushi by Katsuyuki	80.00	80.00				$160.00
Travis Waldron	414.72					$414.72
Weiskopf Consulting	375.00					$375.00
TOTAL	**$3,756.02**	**$1,128.50**	**$241.00**	**$156.00**	**$0.00**	**$5,281.52**

2. Monitor Bills and Expenses

QuickBooks naturally monitors your bills and costs by associating your bank and Visa records to QuickBooks, so the entirety of your costs are downloaded and classified. If you have to follow a check or money exchange, you can record it legitimately in QuickBooks in only a couple of moments.

QuickBooks will also help you with covering your bills when they're expected. For instance, you can guarantee that you pay your bills on time by making an

Accounts Payable Report in less than two minutes. This report will give you the details of your present and past due bills so you can make sure to address any issues rapidly. The following is an example A/P Aging Report from QuickBooks.

Paul's Plumbing
A/P AGING SUMMARY
As of September 30, 2016

	CURRENT	1 - 30	31 - 60	61 - 90	91 AND OVER	TOTAL
Brosnahan Insurance Agency		241.23				$241.23
Diego's Road Warrior Bodyshop	755.00					$755.00
Norton Lumber and Building Mat...		205.00				$205.00
PG&E			86.44			$86.44
Robertson & Associates		315.00				$315.00
TOTAL	$755.00	$761.23	$86.44	$0.00	$0.00	$1,602.67

Sample A/P Aging Summary Report from QuickBooks

3. Increase Key Reporting Insights to Your Business

By dealing with all of your money inflow and outflow exercises in QuickBooks, you can get to a few reports that give significant bits of knowledge into your business. The entirety of the reports are pre-worked in QuickBooks and can be run in only a couple of clicks; reports are refreshed progressively as you enter and save transactions.

This can be useful if you have to give financials to a potential investor or your bank for an independent venture advance or credit extension. Moreover, the Accounts Receivable Report and the Accounts Payable Report that we talked about already, you can run the best three reports that you need to assess the overall health of your business:

- Profit and Loss Report
- Balance Sheet Report
- Statement of Cash Flows

Below, you will locate a concise description of every one of these reports alongside a preview of what it resembles in QuickBooks.

Profit and Loss Report

The benefit and loss report can be run in only several minutes. It will give you how gainful you are by summarizing your salary short of your costs. It shows you your primary concern total compensation (loss) for a particular timeframe, for example, seven days, a month, or a quarter. The following is a Profit and Loss Report for the time of January 1 – September 29, 2016, for a fictitious company, Paul's Plumbing:

Paul's Plumbing Co.
PROFIT AND LOSS
January 1 - September 29, 2016

	TOTAL
Income	
Sales	2,234.00
Services	4,025.00
Total Income	**$6,259.00**
Cost of Goods Sold	
Cost of Goods Sold	750.00
Supplies & Materials - COGS	1,000.00
Total Cost of Goods Sold	**$1,750.00**
Gross Profit	**$4,509.00**
Expenses	
Advertising	8.47
Bank Charges	50.00
Job Materials	2,750.00
Total Expenses	**$2,808.47**
Net Operating Income	**$1,700.53**
Other Income	
Other Income	500.00
Total Other Income	**$500.00**
Net Other Income	**$500.00**
Net Income	**$2,200.53**

Sample Profit and Loss Report from QuickBooks

Balance Sheet Report

The balance sheet report shows the Assets, Liabilities, and Equity for a business at a specific point in time. In only a couple of snaps, you can make a balance sheet report in QuickBooks. The following is a snapshot of a Balance Sheet report as of September 29, 2016, for an invented organization, Paul's Plumbing:

Paul's Plumbing Co.
STATEMENT OF CASH FLOWS
January - September, 2016

	TOTAL
OPERATING ACTIVITIES	
Net Income	2,096.53
Adjustments to reconcile Net Income to Net Cash provided by operations:	
Accounts Receivable	354.00
Inventory Asset	-2,000.00
Accounts Payable	0.00
Bank of America Visa, x7421	300.00
Wells Fargo Credit Card	7,220.20
Total Adjustments to reconcile Net Income to Net Cash provided by operations:	5,874.20
Net cash provided by operating activities	$7,970.73
INVESTING ACTIVITIES	
Truck	-10,000.00
Net cash provided by investing activities	$ -10,000.00
FINANCING ACTIVITIES	
Loan payable - Truck	10,000.00
Opening Balance Equity	2,255.99
Net cash provided by financing activities	$12,255.99
Net cash increase for period	$10,226.72
Cash at beginning of period	5,500.00
Cash at end of period	$15,726.72

Sample Balance Sheet Report from QuickBooks

Statement of Cash Flows

You can rapidly make an announcement of incomes in QuickBooks. This report will give all of you of the exercises that influence the working, contributing, and financing money inflow and cash outflow for your business. The following is a preview of the announcement of incomes for the period January, September 2016 for an invented organization, Paul's Plumbing:

Sample Statement of Cash Flows Report from QuickBooks

4. Run Payroll

Payroll is a region that you would prefer not to hold back on by attempting to do it manually. Mistakes made in figuring checks can bring about steep punishments and unhappy. To help, QuickBooks has its very own payroll work that can consequently figure and run payroll as regularly as you need it.

The best part about utilizing QuickBooks payroll is that it is coordinated with QuickBooks, so your budget reports are consistently state-of-the-art as of the most recent payroll run. The acquisition of a QuickBooks payroll membership is required with the goal that you approach the most recent payroll charge tables to figure representative and business payroll charges.

A portion of the advantages of running payroll with QuickBooks are:

- Pay representatives with a check or direct store
- Federal and state payroll charges are determined naturally

- QuickBooks fills in the payroll tax documents for you
- You can e-pay directly from QuickBooks

5. Track Inventory

If you have to monitor the stock you sell, for example, close by sums and unit costs, QuickBooks will naturally track and refresh this for you as you enter exchanges. In QuickBooks, there are a few reports accessible to manage inventory.

While monitoring inventory is possible in an Excel spreadsheet, it tends to be very time-consuming. The following is an example Inventory Valuation Summary Report from

QuickBooks. This report shows a list of your stock items, the amount available, normal expense, and their total worth.

6. Improve Taxes

In case you're as yet not convinced that you can simplify your charges by utilizing QuickBooks, consider the amount you fear the charge season. Regardless of whether you need to unite a few Excel spreadsheets or organize a shoebox full of receipts, it can take you longer to get your tax professional what they need than it takes to set up your government form!

Here at Fit Small Business, we use QuickBooks Online to deal with the entirety of our business accounting and taxes. We have set up our tax professional with a client id and secret key to get to our QuickBooks information and pull the data they have to document our assessment forms. Since everything is followed in QuickBooks, we don't invest a great deal of energy sorting out receipts and bank statements. This not just guarantees that we have represented all salaries and costs, yet it also improves accuracy as a result.

7. Accept Online Payments

Perhaps the ideal approach to improve your income is to offer clients the choice to pay their invoices on the web. With QuickBooks, you can include the Intuit Payments feature with a simple click of a button.

When activated, all client invoices that you send using the email will incorporate a "Pay Now" button. Your client can tap on that catch and pay their receipt utilizing any significant charge card or by entering their bank balance data to approve an ACH installment directly from their ledger.

There is no month to month expense to utilize Intuit Payments; you pay per exchange as follows:

- Bank Transfers (ACH) – Free
- Card Swiped – 2.4% in addition to 25 pennies
- Card Invoiced – 2.9% in addition to 25 pennies
- Card Keyed-in – 3.4% in addition to 25 pennies

8. Scan Receipts

Another vital aspect of making charge time a breeze has the option to sort out your receipts in QuickBooks. All QBO subscribers can download the QuickBooks App to their cell phone for nothing, click a photo of a receipt, and transfer it to QBO in only a couple of moments.

Not any more lost receipts or physically coordinating up receipts with downloaded banking exchanges. QuickBooks enables you to append a receipt to the comparing banking exchange! You can transfer an unlimited number of receipts to QBO to store in the cloud alongside your information. This can be extremely useful for organizations that track many costs, similar to lawyers and law offices.

Why pick QuickBooks

QuickBooks has a few competitors:

- Xero
- FreshBooks
- Sage 50 (Previously known as Peachtree)
- Account Edge
- Wave
- Others…

Furthermore, individuals consistently ask me the magic inquiry: "Why QuickBooks and not another program?" or "Other than QuickBooks, what are my decisions for an accounting program?"

Presently, because I am NOT a client of whatever another program that isn't QuickBooks, I can't make a feature by features comparison, however, I will refer to the bullet points as of why I prescribe

QuickBooks blindly to nearly my customers instead of investigating another arrangement:

- QuickBooks comes in a few "flavors": QuickBooks Online Simple Start, QuickBooks Online Essentials, QuickBooks Online Plus, QuickBooks Mac, QuickBooks Pro, QuickBooks Premier, and QuickBooks Enterprise. So we have a ton of adaptability in evaluating, includes, and preferred mode of work. With both a CLOUD arrangement and a DESKTOP arrangement.
- Mobile and iPad similarity: both Online and Windows versions have an alternative to cell phone and tablet interfaces (restricted obviously) for certain exchanges out and about.
- Online Banking (Bank Fees): virtually every bank in the US has a QuickBooks trade alternative, which accelerates the information section and bank compromise exponentially versus 100% manual information section frameworks. Some accounting programs don't have these features.
- Accountant Support: most CPA's and Tax preparers out in the open practice support QuickBooks and can get a QB document to play out their work. Other accounting frameworks may not be friendly to work with littler or non-particular CPA firms. Additionally, accountants get a specific arrangement of tools from Accountant's form of QuickBooks that accelerate the accounting process

- Several QuickBooks Consultants: there are 60k in addition to individuals from the Intuit ProAdvisor Network, and it's simple to discover nearby experts all over the US to enable the clients to arrange/arrangement or backing QuickBooks.

- Community Support: If you search "QuickBooks instructional exercise" on YouTube, you will discover a huge number of recordings to learn QuickBooks all alone. The Intuit Support site: http://support.quickbooks.intuit.com/has huge amounts of technical information. The people group Support site: https://community.intuit.com/has additionally huge amounts of Q&As commonly asked and replied by clients.

- Local Training: like us, there are numerous nearby advisors and Community Colleges educating QuickBooks courses, and no other accounting program

- 3rd Party Apps: QuickBooks hosts the biggest database of third gathering good applications that import and fare information among QuickBooks and non-accounting different frameworks like CRM, Workflow Management, Shopping Carts, Inventory, and so on.

- Payroll Support: there are many accounting programs that don't have Payroll Support, or its a manual procedure. QuickBooks has EFTPS installment computerization, and IRS structure filling worked in.

- Feel Safer—We abhor accepting that telephone call that a customer's Pro or Premier record has kept them out of their organization document, and we have to have the record fixed by Intuit–and they need to move up to QuickBooks Enterprise at any rate! Check your record size by pressing ctrl + 1. If you are moving toward 80,000KB - 100,000KB, the time has come to begin taking a look at Premier from Pro. By 100,000KB to 120,000KB, it is the ideal opportunity for you to climb to Enterprise.

- Help When You Need It – A unique offer included for one year, ES offers access to U.S. - based item specialists, unlimited specialized help, upgrades, and online backup.
- Employee Organizer – Use the implicit HR instrument to follow contract dates, fire dates, raises, expected a set of responsibilities, and even notes with a period and date stamp to follow representative issues.
- Price/Value: I don't have the pricing idea about the definite evaluating of all the accounting programs out there, however the number of features versus value correlation. You can purchase QuickBooks Pro for about $180 from Amazon or QuickBooksPrice.com, and it commonly keeps going three years without the requirement for an upgrade.
- QuickBooks is incredibly adaptable and takes into account every business to customize it to fit explicit needs. From following stock levels to making singular measures and invoices, QuickBooks adjusts to your special utilization of the program.

- Many simple accounting assignments can be consequently recorded in the product, which spares you important time and effort. For instance, numerous banks and Visas will connect to QuickBooks and download your exchanges, dispensing with manual passage and mistakes.
- Because the installed client base of QuickBooks is so broad, the item has been generally tried and is entirely steady and reliable. At the point when you look at all the functionality and features of this product in connection to its expense, there is essentially no other item in the market at this level, which offers a superior incentive for the private business enterprise.
- QuickBooks is perfect with numerous vertical market applications that permit industry afterward programming applications to export directly into QuickBooks, and a greater amount of these applications are being incorporated constantly. Models include Point of Sale, Construction, and Medical and so on. Also, the QuickBooks Premier Edition has been expanded into explicit industry versions.
- Realizing that numerous private companies have or before long will exceed the capacities of QuickBooks, Intuit released its cutting edge programming called QuickBooks Enterprise Solutions, which enables a lot bigger business associations to utilize the item. For instance, QuickBooks Enterprise Solutions is a superior fit for a business with maybe 100 to 200

- representatives, $10 million in deals with arranging access to up to 20 simultaneous clients.
- QuickBooks gives various exceptional reports that can be effectively made at whatever point you need to perceive how your business is getting along. The entirety of your records meets up here to show you a general perspective on your business health.
- Save cash by utilizing QuickBooks. You are picking affordable programming that encourages you to deal with all parts of your business in a financially good way.
- The client base behind QuickBooks demonstrates that it is reliable, well-established accounting software. A huge number of organizations everywhere throughout the world have picked QuickBooks, and the quantity of clients keeps on developing.
- QuickBooks enables information to be imported from numerous well-known applications like the Microsoft Office Suite. Independent company applications and additional items have also been made to coordinate data consistently into your QuickBooks programming.
- QuickBooks can help develop your business by creating a strategy to keep you on track and arrive at your objectives. This arrangement can be utilized to obtain small business credit or sort out assets for future extensions.

QuickBooks, similar to any accounting programming, is just a tool. Similarly, as the purchase of carpentry tools won't transform a novice into a fine specialist, neither one of the wills accounting programming independent from anyone else viably deal with your business. In such a manner, similarly, as with most abilities, there is no substitute for information and experience. My QuickBooks programming information is commended by long experience of involvement with bookkeeping and money related detailing, tax assessment, and business advisory services over a wide scope of projects. This gives me an unparalleled bit of benefit in helping you - the entrepreneur - actualize a fruitful QuickBooks arrangement for your organization.

Among the manners in which I can assist you with QuickBooks include:

- Installing programming, arrangement, and plan of suitable bookkeeping accounting for your business.
- Issues related to introducing and running QuickBooks in multi-client mode on a system.
- You are developing or altering a current diagram of records that is appropriate for your business.
- Determining to open adjusts - not constantly a simple procedure, particularly if you are changing over from a manual bookkeeping framework.
- I am reconciling a point of interest receivable, payable, stock and finance registers to the general record.
- I am outlining an organized change procedure to make progress from your current framework to QuickBooks.

- ➢ I am setting up client, seller, stock, finance, and employment costing records and layout documents.
- ➢ I am customizing structures and reports.
- ➢ Fixed resource valuable detailing.
- ➢ I am integrating vertical market applications with QuickBooks.
- ➢ Reviewing your current QuickBooks arrangement and offering recommendations for development.
- ➢ You are training your staff in QuickBooks.
- ➢ Providing an occasional total survey of your exchanges and general record and making revisions where vital.
- ➢ You are providing continuous warning help to your business on an "as required" basis or for ventures requiring extraordinary expertise in bookkeeping, tax assessment, planning, etc.

Picking the right QuickBooks plan

Not certain which variant of QuickBooks you ought to pick? Can't choose if QuickBooks Online, QuickBooks Desktop, or some other variant of QuickBooks is directly for your business?

With five distinct items to look over, choosing the best QuickBooks programming can be tough. Also, the way that QuickBooks isn't generally the most expected with data about their items!

In this total QuickBooks Comparison, we'll clarify what each program is prepared to do, what sort of business is best for every adaptation of QuickBooks, and the principle contrasts between every item. We'll additionally walk you through what inquiries to pose so you can pinpoint the ideal QuickBooks programming for your business and pick the privilege QuickBooks bookkeeping arrangement with confidence.

Try not to have the opportunity to read our full correlation post? The following chart separates the fundamental contrasts between QuickBooks Online, QuickBooks Pro, QuickBooks Premier, QuickBooks Enterprise, and QuickBooks Self-Employed.

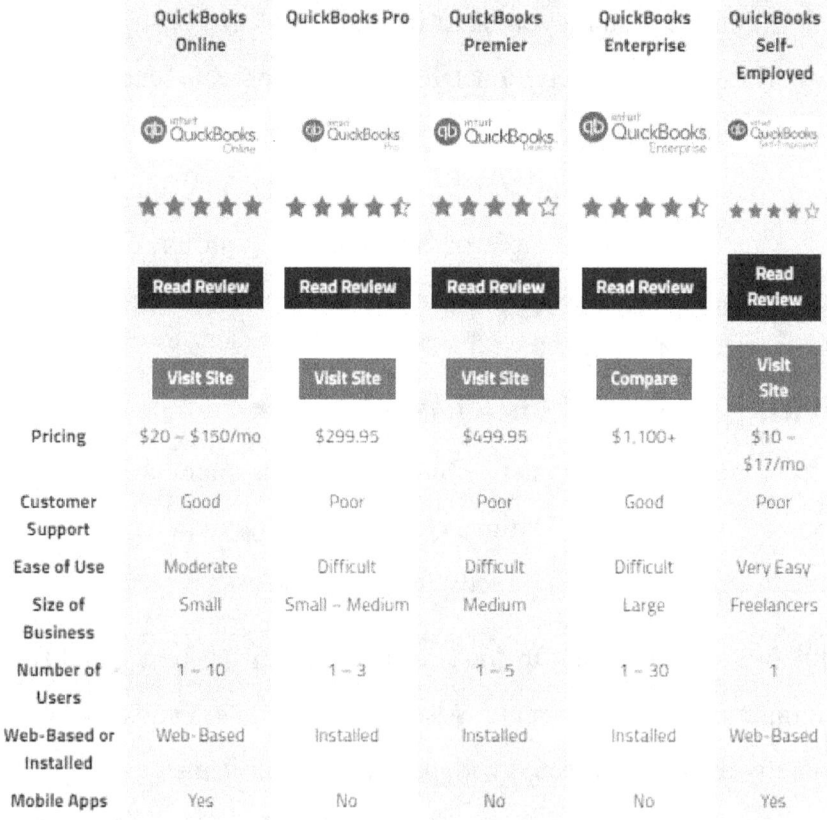

Diagram of QuickBooks Products

QuickBooks Online

Launched in 2004, QuickBooks Online is cloud-based bookkeeping programming utilized by more than 2 million individuals. With solid bookkeeping capacities, amazing features, and completely included mobile applications, it's no big surprise; this is one of our main 5/5 star bookkeeping suggestions.

Best for...

Small companies without any than 25 clients searching for a simple to utilize cloud-based accounting programming and strong mobile applications.

Pricing

QuickBooks Online (QBO) offers three estimating plans running from $20 – $150/month. The bigger the arrangement, the more features you approach, and the more clients are permitted. The biggest arrangement incorporates ten clients (although you can have up to 25 clients until 7/31/2019). Payroll costs an extra $35/mo-$80/month +plus $4/month per representative). Fortunately, Intuit is quite often running a business advancement. Read our total QuickBooks Online audit for all the pricing details.

Features

QuickBooks Online offers several automation and features. The product considers every contingency just as invoicing, cost following, creditor liabilities, contact management, project management, and the sky is the limit from there. Even though there are occasional route troubles, QBO is unbelievably simple to utilize generally.

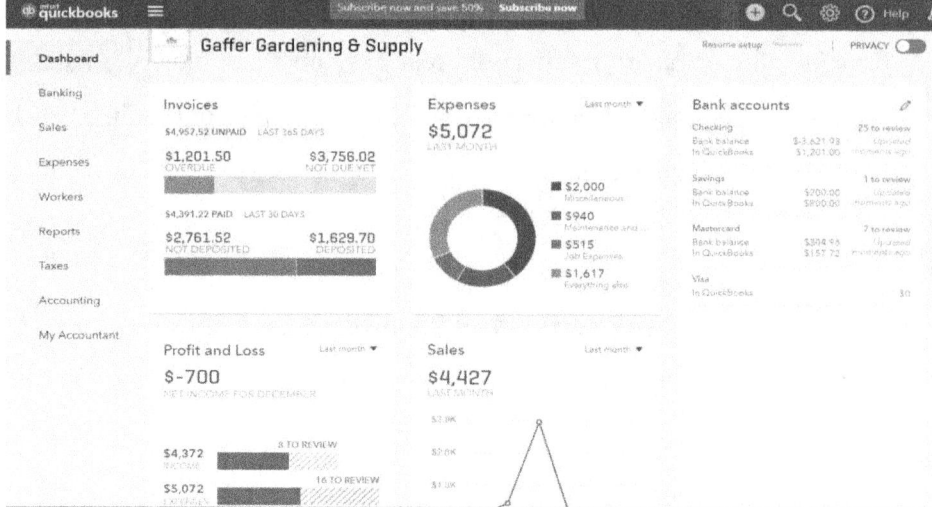

Something that truly sets QuickBooks separated from other bookkeeping items is its new loaning highlight — QuickBooks Capital. QuickBooks Capital uses the data as of now in QuickBooks Online to decide if a small business is qualified for a loan.

A portion of our other most loved features include:

- Invoice planning
- Class following
- Inventory
- Time following
- Print checks

QBO offers more than 550 reconciliations, which is the majority of any QuickBooks item.

QuickBooks is commonly known for poor client support, yet QuickBooks Online has is working of late to restore its notoriety by shortening long hold up times and upgrading their assistance focus.

If incorporations, convenience, and portability are essential to you, QuickBooks Online is your most logical option. If you need to perceive how QuickBooks Online stacks facing different QuickBooks items, keep reading.

QuickBooks Pro

Launched in 1992, QuickBooks Desktop Pro is the product that set QuickBooks up for life. This 5/5 star programming is privately introduced and offers highly created features.

Best for...

Little to medium-sized business with three clients or less searching for solid accounting or privately introduced programming.

Pricing

There are two pricing choices for QuickBooks Desktop Pro. You can either buy a QuickBooks Pro permit for $299.95 or buy a yearly membership of QuickBooks Pro Plus for $299.95/yr.

If you go with the QuickBooks Pro permit, it will remain current for a long time, after which Intuit drops support for the product. (You can, at present, utilize the product after the three-year point. However, you won't get any help if something goes wrong.) Phone support costs extra.

If you go with QuickBooks Pro Plus, updates and telephone support are incorporated.

Features

As we referenced before, QuickBooks Pro has a mind-blowing number of features. As far as bookkeeping, QuickBooks Pro is one of the most created arrangements accessible, boasting a diagram accounts, diary sections, bank compromise, 130 reports, and then some. These exceptionally created features do have steep learning, however for bookkeepers, those with bookkeeping experience, or the entrepreneur who needs to get their bookkeeping right, setting aside the effort to gain proficiency with the product can pay off.

Best of all, QuickBooks Pro offers many highlights. However, each component is highly created. Intuit thought of everything with this one, even spell-check.

A portion of our other most loved QuickBooks Desktop Pro features include:

- Invoicing
- Project the executives
- Job costing
- Calendar and plan for the day
- Accounts payable
- Budgeting
- Tax support

QuickBooks Pro offers very nearly 200 incorporations, which is a noteworthy number for a privately introduced programming. Not at all like QuickBooks Online, has QuickBooks Pro still experienced poor customer support.

QuickBooks Pro can be an incredible alternative for organizations searching for strong accounting or needing privately introduced programming. The expectation to absorb information makes this product perfect for individuals who have past bookkeeping experience or who are happy to place in an opportunity to get familiar with the product.

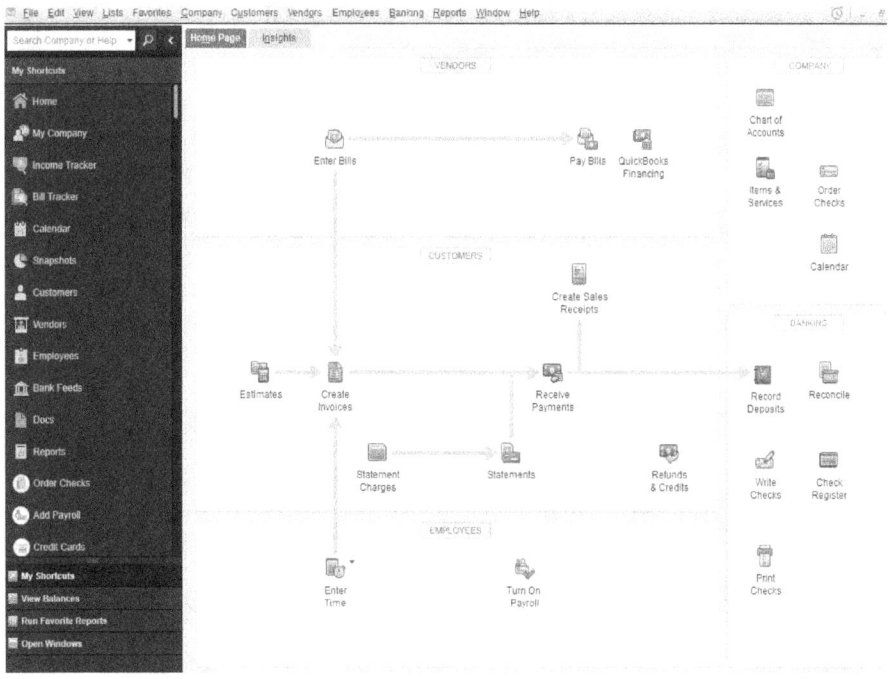

QuickBooks Premier

QuickBooks Desktop Premier is the following stage for medium-sized organizations searching for a similar strong accounting as QuickBooks Pro, yet with more clients and industry-specific features (and a lower cost than QuickBooks Enterprise). Work area Premier is strong, privately introduced programming with many highlights and a decent number of incorporations.

Best for...

Little to medium-sized organizations with five clients or less needing strong accounting and industry-explicit bookkeeping features.

Pricing

QuickBooks Desktop Premier is all the more exorbitant, yet its estimating structure is near indistinguishable from QuickBooks Pros. There are two choices: you can either buy a QuickBooks Premier permit for $499.95 or buy a yearly membership of QuickBooks Premier Plus for $499.95/yr.

If you go with the QuickBooks Premier permit, telephone support costs extra. If you go with QuickBooks Pro Plus, updates and telephone support are incorporated. For the full scoop, visit our Complete Guide to QuickBooks Desktop Pricing.

Features

QuickBooks Premier is advanced for strong accounting. Like QuickBooks Pro, there is a lofty expectation to absorb information here, yet the product incorporates certain features Pro needs, including marketable strategies, stock assemblies, and deals anticipating.

The genuine article that sets QuickBooks Premier separated from QuickBooks Pro is the explicit business highlights. You can pick the standard version of QuickBooks Premier, or you can pick one of five specific releases: Contractor, Manufacturing and Wholesale, Nonprofit, Professional Services, or Retail.

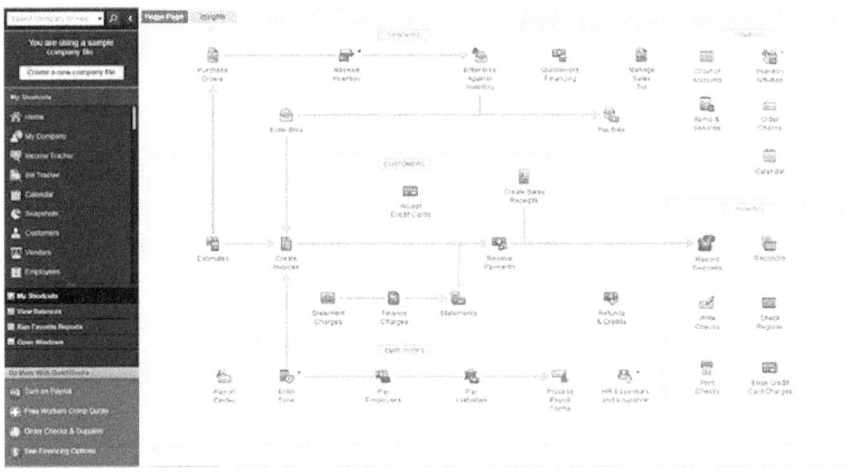

Here are some different features to expect with QuickBooks Desktop Premier:

- Industry-explicit reports
- Sales orders
- Print shipping names

QuickBooks Premier offers 190 incorporations, and client assistance is like that of QuickBooks Pro.

Before choosing QuickBooks Premier, keep perusing for more data. You would prefer not to go through additional cash if the highlights aren't justified, despite any potential benefits.

QuickBooks Enterprise

QuickBooks Desktop Enterprise has a similar incredible accounting capacity of Pro and Premier; however, it permits access for up to 30 clients and significantly more extra room. With six industry-explicit renditions, QuickBooks Enterprise has highly created features to address the issues of almost any enormous business.

Best for…

Huge organizations with 30 clients or less searching for industry-explicit accounting and advanced bookkeeping.

Pricing

QuickBooks Desktop Enterprise features three-yearly memberships: Silver (begins at $1,100/yr), Gold (begins at $1430/yr.), and Platinum (begins at $1,760).

Cost is controlled by the arrangement you select and the number of clients you have. With QuickBooks Enterprise, you get Intuit Field Management with access for one client. For the full scoop on estimating, read our total QuickBooks Enterprise survey.

Features

As far as features, QuickBooks Enterprise is about as close as you can get to an ERP without doing the change to all-out business the board programming.

Also, the strong bookkeeping you'd expect with a QuickBooks work area item, QuickBooks Enterprise gives invoicing, cost following, contact the executives, project management, work costs, and that's just the beginning.

You can pick the typical adaptation of QuickBooks Desktop Enterprise, or you can pick one of the six business explicit versions for included features: Contractor, Manufacturing and Wholesale, Nonprofit, Retail, Professional Services, and Accountant.

Some other notable features include:

- Lead the executives
- Accounts payable
- Inventory
- Business plans
- Loan director
- Tax support

Like QuickBooks Pro, QuickBooks Enterprise also coordinates with about 200 outsider applications.

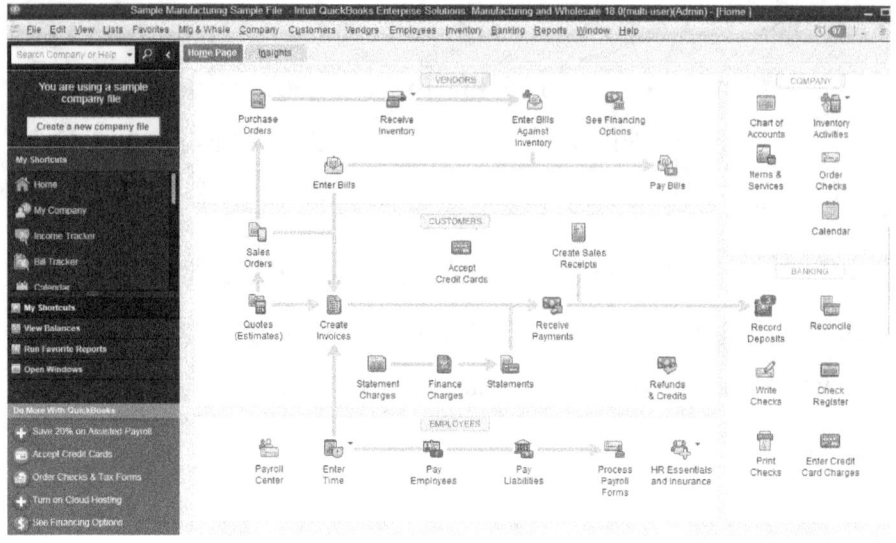

QuickBooks support puts its best foot forward for QuickBooks Enterprise clients. Agents are responsive and friendly, and there are huge amounts of help assets to browse.

That being stated, QuickBooks Enterprise has its disadvantages. The product is amazingly costly, and at the cost, you're paying, certain features like invoicing, project management, time following, and importing are genuinely constrained. Also, the product is more appropriate for huge organizations than enterprises, making its name slightly misleading.

QuickBooks Self-Employed

QuickBooks Self-Employed is not the same as the different QuickBooks Products in that it isn't exactly bookkeeping programming. QuickBooks Self-Employed is charge programming made to assist specialists in dealing with their accounts, handle assessed quarterly expenses, and figure reasoning.

Best for...

Freelancers, contractual workers, and other independently employed people are needing essential accounting and expense support.

Pricing

There are two estimating alternatives for QuickBooks Self-Employed. You can either pay $10/mo. For the entirety of the features, QuickBooks Self-Employed brings to the table, or you can pay $17/mo., which will add a Turbo Tax reconciliation to your arrangement.

Intuit is quite often running a business advancement, so make certain to check any potential limits before obtaining. To find out additional, read our total QuickBooks Self-Employed survey.

Features

Like QuickBooks Online, QuickBooks Self-Employed is simple to utilize, cloud-based programming with strong mobile applications. The features are structured explicitly for specialists to address needs like assessment backing and reasoning. You can without much of a stretch separate individual and costs of doing business, which is perfect for specialists who don't have separate business financial balances.

Not exclusively does QuickBooks Self-Employed assist freelancers with exploring the terrifying waters of assessed quarterly charges, it additionally gives them fundamental accounting tools to follow pay and costs.

Here are some different features you can expect with QuickBooks Self-Employed:

- Invoicing
- Fixed resource devaluation
- Schedule Cs
- Tax agenda

QuickBooks Self-Employed has restricted incorporations, yet the Turbo Tax combination is one of the best pieces of the product. At the point when you're prepared to record charges, you can pull the entirety of your QuickBooks Self-Employed information legitimately into Turbo Tax to make documenting simple.

Sadly, QuickBooks Self-Employed's client assistance is much more dreadful than QuickBooks Pro's. There is no telephone support, and extra help assets are restricted. There is a live chat feature and help focus on the event that you need help with.

There is one other downside clients ought to know about: QuickBooks Self-Employed offers government charge support, so you'll need to deal with your state imposes another way.

That being stated, QuickBooks Self-Employed is an incredible choice for freelancers, temporary workers, or other independently employed people. If that is you, you won't locate some other QuickBooks item that is increasingly custom fitted to your particular expense needs.

QuickBooks Online Self-Employed

This adaptation of QuickBooks is intended for specialists. It enables you to:

- Track pay and costs
- Organize receipts
- Estimated charges
- Invoice customers and acknowledge installments
- Track miles
- Run essential reports.

A significant note in regards to the Self-Employed rendition: If you start with this form, you can't move up to some other arrangement. You should begin with one of the small business software forms beneath to have the option to move up to an alternate plan.

QuickBooks Online Simple Start:

This release is expected for private ventures and sole owners. You can easily upgrade to different QuickBooks forms as your business develops.

It offers everything the independently employed form does, in addition to the accompanying features:

- Send measures
- Track deals and deals charge
- Manage 1099 temporary workers

QuickBooks Online Essentials

The following degree of the online programming incorporates the features from Self-Employed and Simple Start, in addition to the accompanying:

- Manage bills
- Track time
- Include three clients

QuickBooks Online Plus

The third degree of online programming propels the accompanying features also what is incorporated with the past version:

- Include five clients
- Track project productivity
- Track stock

QuickBooks Online Advanced

The top-level of online access gives all highlights from the past three releases, in addition to you can:

- Pay bills
- See smart announcing
- Accelerate invoicing
- Create custom client consents and custom fields
- Receive need client support and preparing

Every single online arrangement incorporates application joining, client assistance using instructional exercises and online assets, additional finance items (cost dependent on self-service or full-service in addition to per-representative expense), and a 30-day free trial.

QuickBooks Desktop Pro, Pro Plus and Mac

The work area versions of QuickBooks are introduced on your PC rather than got to on the web. They do exclude software updates except if you pay for the Plus adaptation, which requires a yearly membership charge.

Work area Pro costs a one-time installment and incorporates the accompanying features:

- Track inventory
- Track deals and deals charge
- Send invoices
- Manage bills and records payable
- Track pay and costs

Work area Pro Plus requires a yearly expense and incorporates the product with highlights referenced above in addition to boundless client assistance, information reinforcement and recovery, and access to software updates.

QuickBooks for Mac is like Pro, in spite of the fact that not actually since it offers a few features upgraded for the Mac stage (even though QuickBooks' site doesn't determine which includes these are).

Pro and Pro, also, to empower fare to Excel and reconciliation with Outlook; Mac empowers fare to Apple Numbers programming, just as the capacity to later change over to Online or Windows programming.

QuickBooks Desktop Premier and Premier Plus

The Premier degree of QuickBooks' work area programming, which requires a one-time installment, incorporates the entirety of the usefulness of QuickBooks Pro in addition to the accompanying extra features:

- See industry-explicit reports
- Create deals orders
- Track costs for items and stock

- Customize stock reports
- Support up to five clients

The Premier Plus version, as with the Pro Plus adaptation, permits unlimited client care, robotized information reinforcement and recovery, and access to the most recent software updates. It requires a yearly membership expense too.

How to Choose the Right Version of QuickBooks for Your Business

If you read the diagram of each QuickBooks item, you may, as of now, have a thought of which adaptation of QuickBooks is best for your small business. If not, don't stress. These five inquiries will assist you with narrowing down your inquiry and find what you're searching for.

Do You Want Cloud-Based or Locally-Installed Software?

The principal significant central factor is whether you need cloud-based or locally-installed software.

Cloud-based programming works totally in the cloud (on the web). A few advantages of cloud-based programming include:

- Mobility
- Access for numerous clients in various areas
- SaaS membership-based evaluating model
- Security is dealt with by the product supplier
- Usually accompanies mobile applications

Locally-installed software is downloaded and introduced on a solitary, on-premise PC. A few advantages of locally-installed software include:

- No web get to required
- More complex and feature-rich
- Potentially increasingly secure (you are answerable for security)

Most small businesses lean toward cloud-based programming as it is increasingly moderate, simpler to utilize, and stays aware of our general society's mobile way of life. Nonetheless, locally-installed software can be increasingly secure and offers a degree of feature depth that the cloud regularly can't contact.

Choosing which kind of programming works best for your plan of action can settle on your QuickBooks decision a mess simpler. If you need cloud-based programming, there's QuickBooks Online and QuickBooks Self-Employed. If you need locally-installed software, you can take your pick from QuickBooks Pro, QuickBooks Premier, or QuickBooks Enterprise.

Are You A Mac or Windows User?

QuickBooks Pro, Premier, and Enterprise are altogether intended for Windows. So in case, you're a Mac client, you're down to two alternatives: QuickBooks Online and QuickBooks Enterprise.

What Type Of Business Do You Run?

The sort of business you run effects which QuickBooks item is directly for you. In case you're a specialist, QuickBooks Self-Employed is the undeniable decision. In case you're maintaining a small business, you'll be looking at QuickBooks Online or QuickBooks Pro.

Bigger organizations will take a gander at QuickBooks Premier or QuickBooks Enterprise, contingent upon the number of clients they need.

What number of Users Do You Need?

The number of clients you need will also help figure out which programming is best for your business. Investigate this graph to see which item suits your business' size.

QuickBooks Self-Employed:	1 user
QuickBooks Pro:	1 – 3 users
QuickBooks Premier:	1 – 5 users
QuickBooks Online:	1 – 25 users
QuickBooks Enterprise:	1 – 30 users

Note: This diagram shows the most extreme number of clients available with every version of QuickBooks, which may cost extra.

The amount Accounting Experience Do You Have?

If you don't think a lot about bookkeeping, you'll need to avoid QuickBooks Pro, Premier, or Enterprise, except if you're willing to place in an opportunity to learn.

QuickBooks Online and QuickBooks Self-Employed are much simpler choices to get a handle if you don't have much understanding or need to continue adjusting the books.

Then again, in case you're an accountant or somebody with much accounting experience, you may like the difficulty of the QuickBooks work area alternatives as they stick to progressively traditional accounting practices.

1. Find an accountant.

Before you begin, the principal thing you need to do is talk about relocating your funds to QuickBooks with a trusted financial professional. For this, Intuit offers an online accountant coordinating assistance called ProAdvisor. However, most accountants support the administration so that a nearby referral can fill in too.

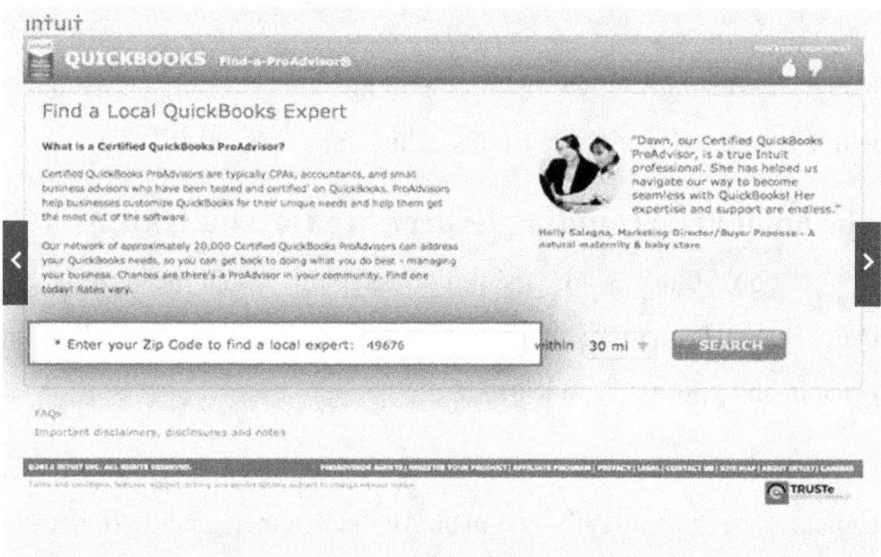

The reason: a telephone discussion or email trade with the accountant to decide and confirm the points of interest about your business that QuickBooks needs, including your business structure, the right shows for following costs, and your commitments in regards to state or local regulators.

2. Review the QuickBooks basics.

Presently, become familiar with the product. Regardless of whether you are alright with numbers, invest energy in the "Beginning" tab on the instructional exercises that present how QuickBooks' ponders dealing with the bills you send and get and your association's expenses. QuickBooks arranges income as "Cash In," and costs as "Cash Out." It, at that point, maps the progression of these assets through your business in a chart called "Getting Around."

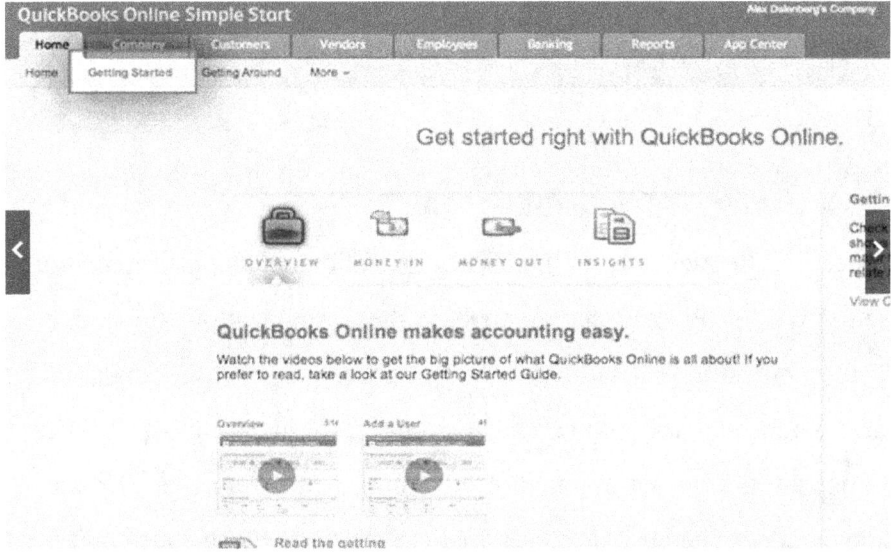

3. Set up a secure environment.

Security is basic whenever cash is in question, and especially so with QuickBooks because your whole money related life is in one spot. Before you start entering sensitive financial data, go to the "Change Password" tab in the "Your Account" area, and make a one of a kind and complex password. You also need to consider changing this and the passwords that QuickBooks stores, your web-based financial IDs at your bank's site, and in QuickBooks, each quarter.

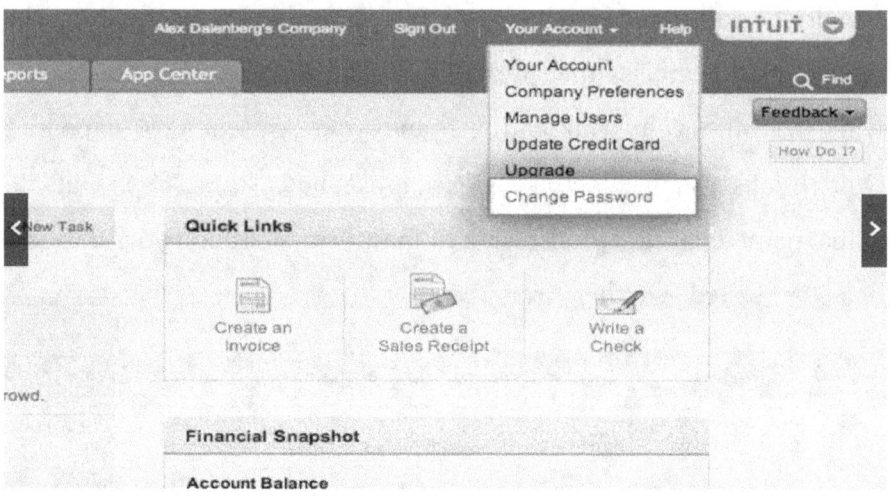

4. Enter your business vitals.

Since you know about the QuickBooks rudiments and your passwords set, go to the "Preferences" connect in the "Organization" tab and enter your organization's details regarding finance, in light of the fundamental discussions you had with your accountant. As a rule, the most significant things are the business structure, revealing structures, Tax ID number, and detailed schedule. However, that can fluctuate by business, and even minor details can be basic. Consider twofold checking these details with your financial advisor by telephone or email.

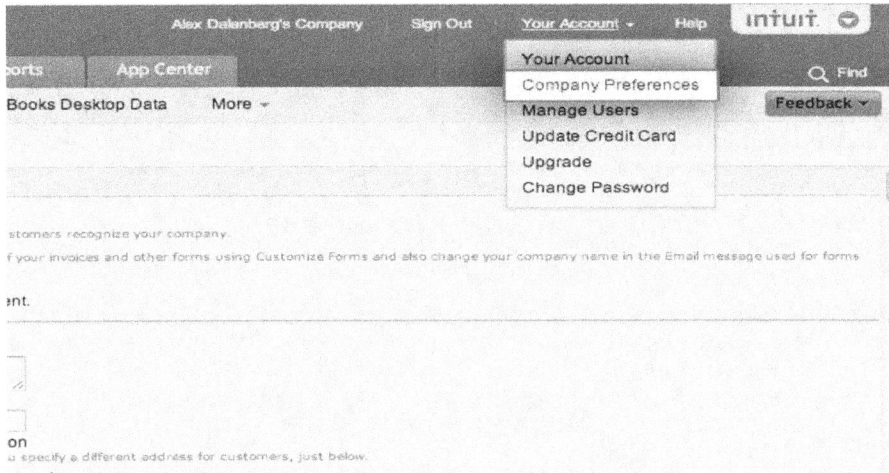

5. Enter client data.

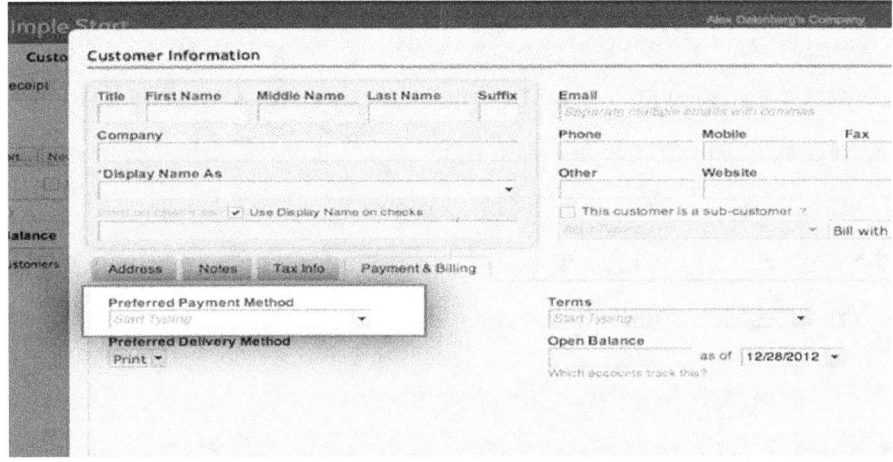

Presently, head to the "Client" tab and start entering customer data. While the name, address, and email are significant, the basic component is the "Installment Method" choice. Check with your clients directly to decide if they lean toward paying with money, check, or Visa. At that point, set the choices as required and, if conceivable, create a test receipt for your customers. Affirm with them that all fills in as it should.

6. Enter essential seller and representative data.

```
QuickBooks Online Simple Start
  Home      Company      Customers      Vendors      Employees      Banking
  Vendor List    Manage Bills    More ▾

Vendor Information

    Full Name...              >  |
    Company
    Display Name As
    Print on Check As
    Address
                                                              Map
    Street

    City                                            State
    ZIP Code                          Country
```

Next, go to the "Vendors" and "Employees" tabs. Start by entering the contact data for who works for you and who offers to you; however, don't feel constrained to enter all of the detail that QuickBooks prompts. Confirm every section by creating a report with the "Report" button on the privilege of the screen. Now, there shouldn't be a requirement for alternatives; for example, "Oversee Bills" or "Finance."

7. Start following the cash stream.

Presently comes the tricky part: representing the genuine dollars your business makes and spends. For this, dive into the "Banking" tab and focus on the essential revealing alternatives to follow the cash you make and the costs your business acquires. You can associate with most applicable budgetary records, for example, ledgers and credit cards from here.

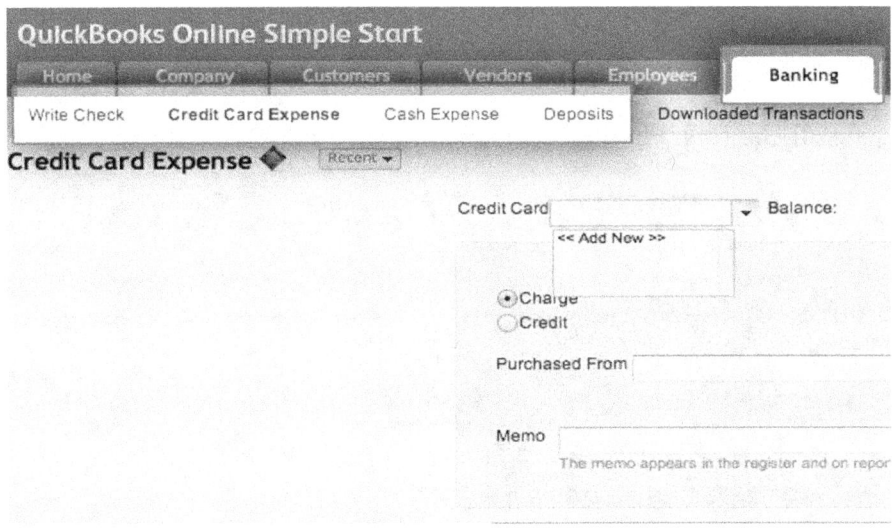

Be certain you can cut checks with the "Write Checks" tab and deal with your expenses and deals in the "Credit card Expense," "Money Expense," and "Store" headings. Do a trial run with every one of these highlights to ensure that you comprehend them effectively, and QuickBooks is recording the information appropriately.

You'll also need to deal with the movement for you. You can utilize the "Oversee Users" screen, situated in the "Your Account" area, to include clients, preferably just yourself and your accountant, and to see "Movement" reports that show which includes doing what inside the account.

8. Review expense labels and confirm them with a bookkeeper.

Business finds it must be sorted out by classification for both expense purposes and controllers. Along these lines, you'll have to know the stray pieces of describing what your business spends. Make certain to see how to follow "Money Expenses" by hand versus, consequently, downloading cost information from a bank or Reddit account, which can generally be found in the "Downloaded Transactions" segment.

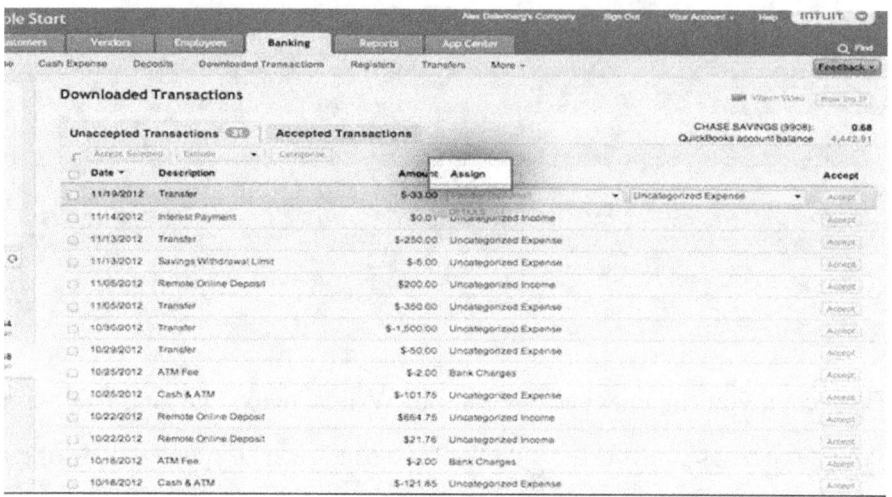

Physically entering money costs into QuickBooks can be a generally simple procedure. Enter an amount, relegate a seller, and join a notice. Cost information from bank or Visa records can be uploaded automatically. Once more, it's most likely a smart thought to confirm with an accountant early on that you are naming these accurately.

9. Create your first profit and loss report.

Since you've looked into your cost marks, it's an ideal opportunity to decide how much cash your business makes. Intuit has a full arrangement of revealing instruments in any case, for the present, focus on the "Benefit and Loss" report found in the "Report" tab. The Profit and Loss report includes what you made for a period and afterward subtracts the costs you brought about dependent on the information entered in QuickBooks. In addition to other things, the report can help give you a thought of the money you'll require close by to pay imposes on your potential benefit.

Also, Intuit offers a "Retain" work that makes it simple to catch this and other explicit reports all the time and show them to your accountant.

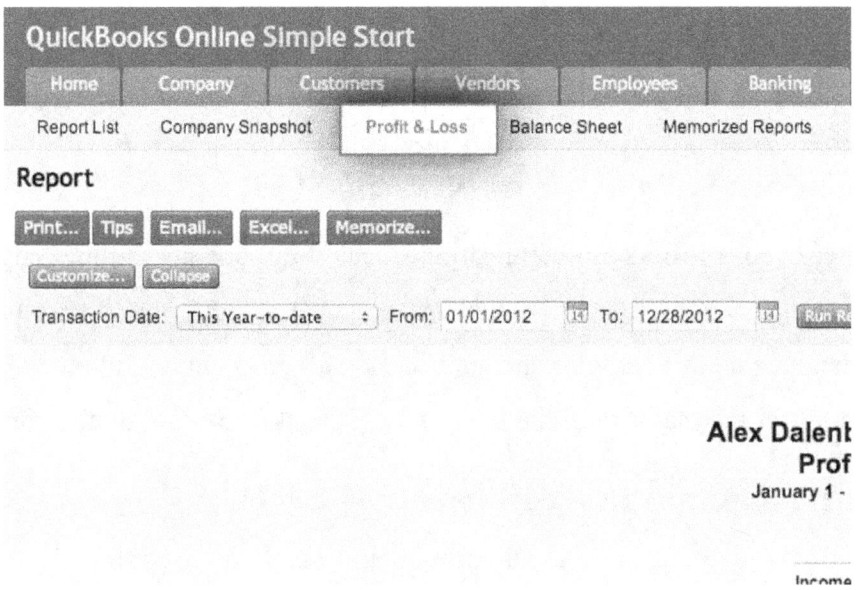

10. Include features as required.

When you have the nuts and bolts down, invoicing, deals following, cost checking and deciding benefit or loss and expense commitments, you can begin including features. Your following stages may incorporate making an essential accounting report, investigating your announcement of incomes, and automating how you reconcile your bank statements.

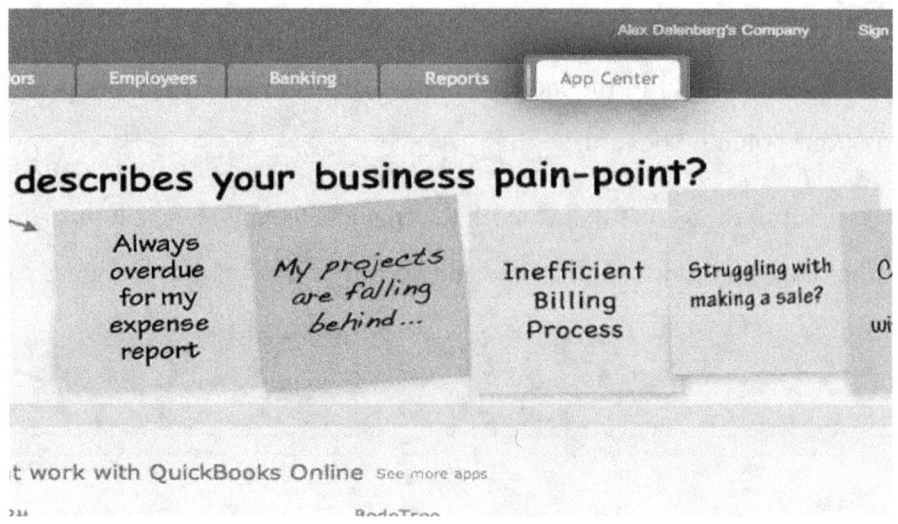

QuickBooks offers an application focus to work in cutting edge instruments for client relationships, the board, stock, and charging. There are additionally mobile applications for Android and iPhone that empower the majority of the fundamental QuickBooks online features.

Including your first customer...

Did you realize that you can consolidate both your Desktop and your online clients to QuickBooks Online Accountant? To include the work area customers, it's moderately simple. Explore to your books and then go to deals and client and include the customer.

Including an online client is extremely simple, as well. You should request that the client include you as an accountant user. With my CRM (client relationship the board program), 17 caps, I have preset layouts.

At the point when a customer connects with me using my contact form, I utilize a work process to send them a template email requesting access.

The verbiage of the email appeared below advises the customer to go to the tools, account settings, oversee clients, bookkeeping firm. Afterward, include my email address. It's direct. If a customer battles with this, I have a video demonstrating this procedure. I attempt to keep it as direct as workable for the individual that may turn into a potential customer.

Including an accountant user...

Once invited, I acknowledge the welcome from the email I got as the accountant. Regularly, this progression is only a couple of clicks. In any case, as you'll find in the video below, it doesn't fill in as arranged. One recommendation is to ensure that you don't have any examples of anything Intuit opens in the program. When we shut everything down and then re-click the welcome, I had the option to get to the customer.

Moreover, here is the authority pdf on the most proficient method to change over a record from QuickBooks' work area to QuickBooks on the web. Make certain to follow every one of them. Try not to avoid any. Here are some key points:

Our Conversion Tips...

1. Make sure to set up the work area record first. Accommodate up to the nearest date conceivable. This is a significant advance to prepare the record before you process it.

2. I recommend making a convenient document of your work area record and later re-establishing that as you're working document. This will be the document that you will change over. Making a versatile

record puts the work area document in an excellent request. I know it's an additional progression. However, it's basic to ensure you have a pleasant, sound stable record for a change.

3. When the information is changed over, make certain to re-accommodate the latest relevant point of interest. For the online document, you need to make one major compromise to re-accommodate it back to where it was in Desktop.

4. Run a trial parity in both the work area in the online versions. Make certain to confirm the information by utilizing the date extend all in the detailing basis accrual.

Thoughts on Wholesale Billing...

This is the place we settle on disagree. At Parkway business arrangements, Matthew and the group incorporate all memberships and applications in their evaluation to the customer. They pack everything.

At Artisan Bookkeeping, this was my strategy. With the ongoing change in not having the option to include existing customers the discount charging and get the half-off advantage, I chose to move my outlook. Presently, I have removed the QuickBooks on the web and full-service payroll subscriptions from the group. This gives the customer a chance to pay that straightforwardly. I was encountering customer pushback at a year-end audit with my clients. Regularly, I would hear, "I paid you that much for accounting?" The customer would overlook that the memberships a packaged in there. I have them pay it directly.

Try not to let my method for estimating (non-packaging) dissuade you from utilizing discount charging or packaging. Discount charging is an extraordinary advantage that you can go along to your new customer, particularly if they're not in QuickBooks online when they come to you. If they come to you and have no accounting software, don't hesitate to include them in and give them the markdown. You can also keep it for yourself and incorporate that when you are evaluating the activity.

Make sure to get settled in advance. I feel compelled to pressure that as much as possible. Take it from somebody who didn't do it and stalled out a couple of times. Any work you do in QuickBooks, in their program, is the customers at one time the activity is finished. If you don't get paid ahead of time and they don't pay you, there's nothing you can do about it.

This is only the best business practice. If they're hesitant to pay you upfront, offer to have them pay you with a charge card. They can generally return to the credit card organization by contesting the charge. When you instruct the customer about this, it typically will remove their fear of prepaying.

A quick preview of next week...

So we trust these tips were useful as we begin to get further into the program, and the various advantages included QuickBooks Online Accountant. One week from now will address the preparation for you and your customer, and we will get into taking a look at getting confirmed by stepping through the exam and the entirety of the incredible instructive bits of turning into a ProAdvisor. We can't pressure enough that it is so critical to step through the exam and step through the Advanced examination to raise every other person. It'll likewise get you recorded on the discover a ProAdvisor site. That will produce leads. We will discuss our onboarding forms (they are very extraordinary!) and applications!

Basic Steps to Operating QuickBooks

Bookkeepers and accountants regularly ask me what they ought to do first to familiarize themselves with their customers' QuickBooks® Online records. Have confidence; it's not as daunting as it might appear. Here are my ten key strides to getting settled with QuickBooks Online.

1. Get familiar with the Layout

In contrast to traditional desktop software, QuickBooks Online is available over various gadgets and working frameworks, much like an application you'd use on a cell phone or tablet. In case you're familiar with desktop software, the cloud-based format can take a touch of becoming used to. How about we stroll through it piece by piece.

Dashboard: When you open a customer's organization, the landing page will show you an interactive outline of their Invoices, Sales, Expenses, Profit and Loss, and Bank Accounts.

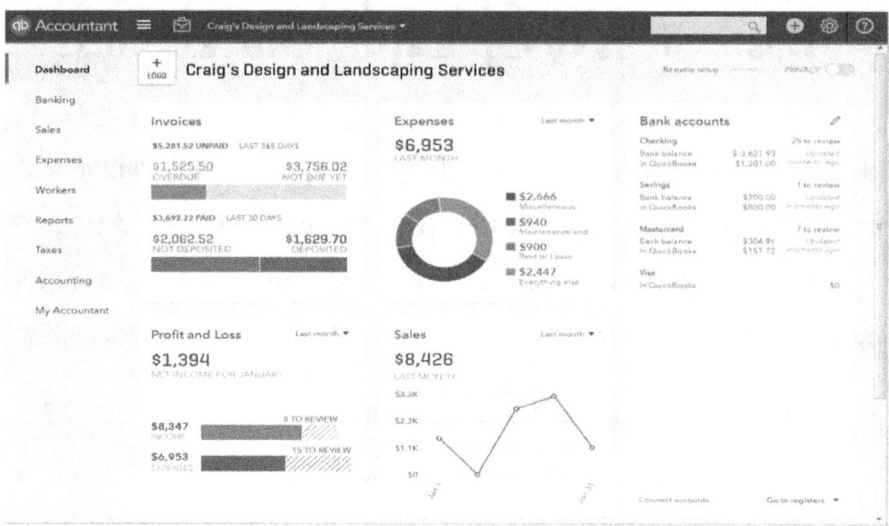

Left navigation: In this board, you'll locate the different tabs you requirement for working in your customers' QuickBooks, separated by class. At the point when you click on a tab, littler subcategories will show up along the top. For instance, by tapping the Sales tab, you can get to these subcategories: All Sales, Invoices, Customers, and Products and Services.

Note: Use the Hamburger symbol (truly, that is the genuine name, even outside of QuickBooks!) to fall and grow the left route to give yourself more space to work.

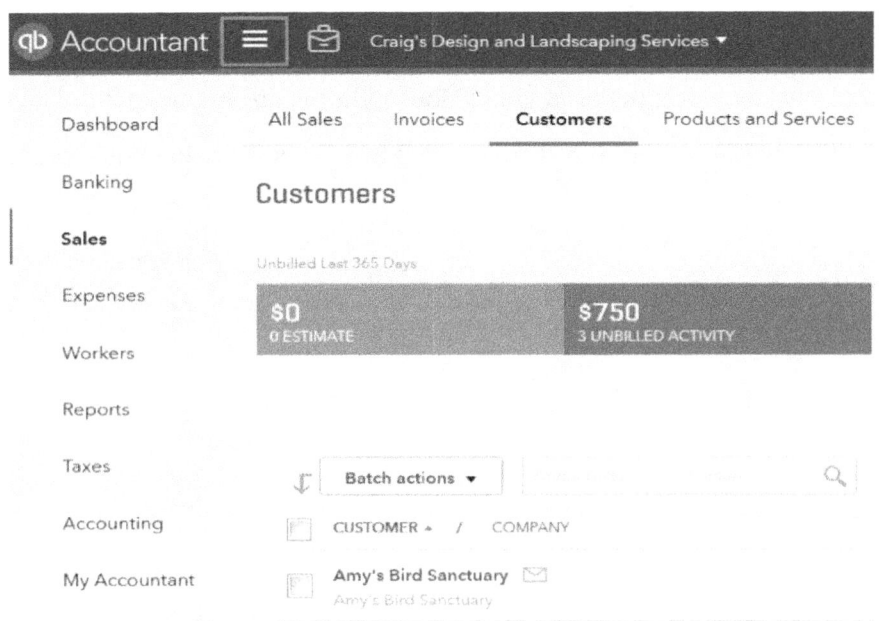

Gear icon: By tapping on the gear symbol in the upper right corner, you'll have the option to get to your customers' Account and Settings, Lists, Tools, and that's just the beginning.

Note: When a little apparatus symbol shows up in the upper corner of a rundown, table, exchange, or report, you'll discover alternatives there to design the settings.

Make (+) symbol: All the kinds of exchanges and exercises you and your customer can make in QuickBooks Online are in one menu. Click the Create (+) symbol beside the search bar to choose what you'd prefer to include.

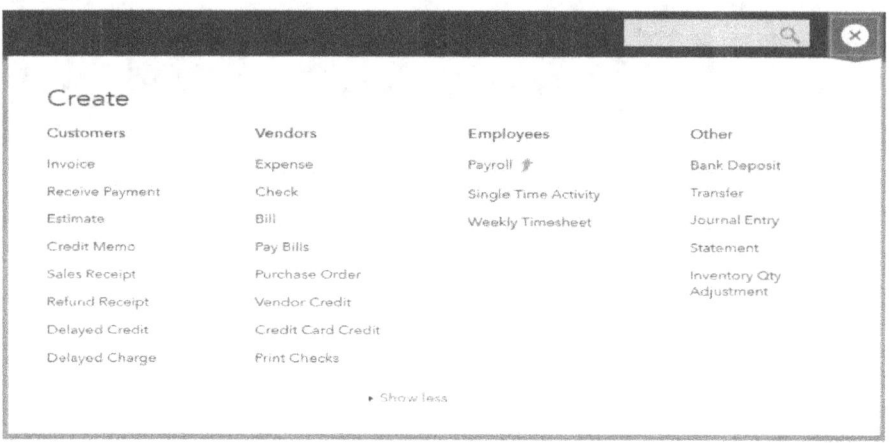

Search bar: The inquiry bar enables you to discover an exchange rapidly. Bookkeepers can also utilize it to open a report or bank account register quickly.

Start typing the name of the report or record. Clicking the search box once will also show a list of ongoing exchanges added to the books.

Note: Use Advanced Search in the base right to fine-tune your search.

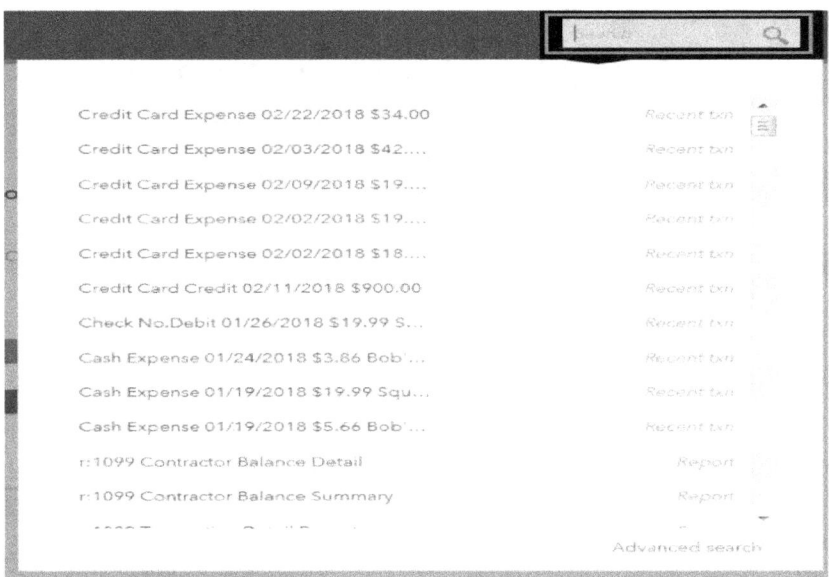

Accountant tool kit: This menu will possibly show up if you are marked as an accountant user. Here, you'll discover instruments that are restrictive to accountants, just as easy routes to the tools and exchanges we think you'll utilize most.

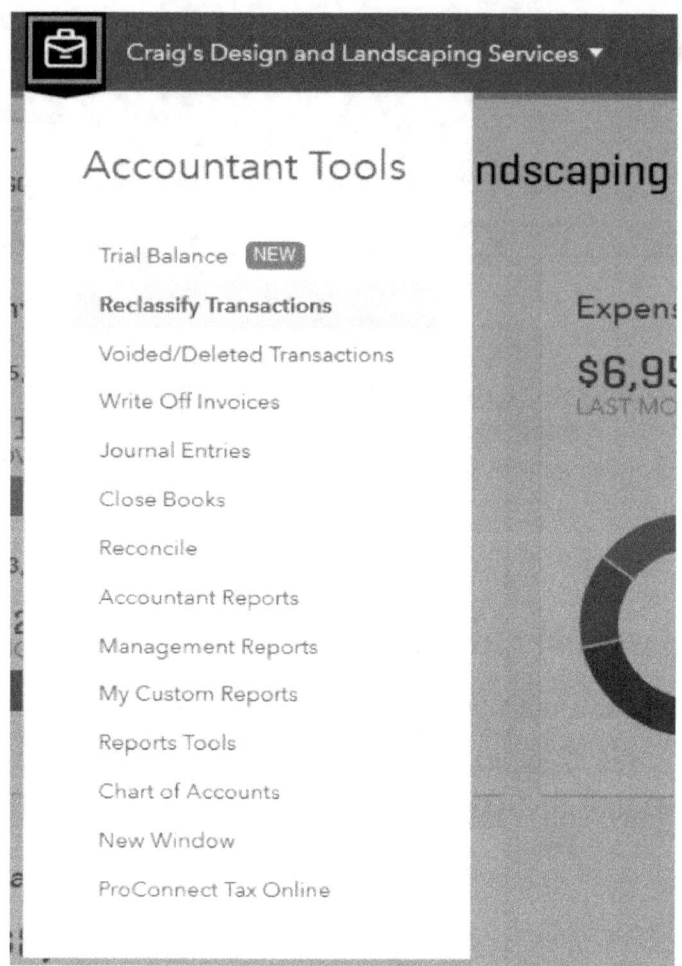

Customer drop-down: As an accountant, you can toggle back between customers or hop into your training by tapping on the customer drop-down list. If you have an extensive list of customers, rapidly hop to the one you're searching for by composing the organization name in the Find a customer field.

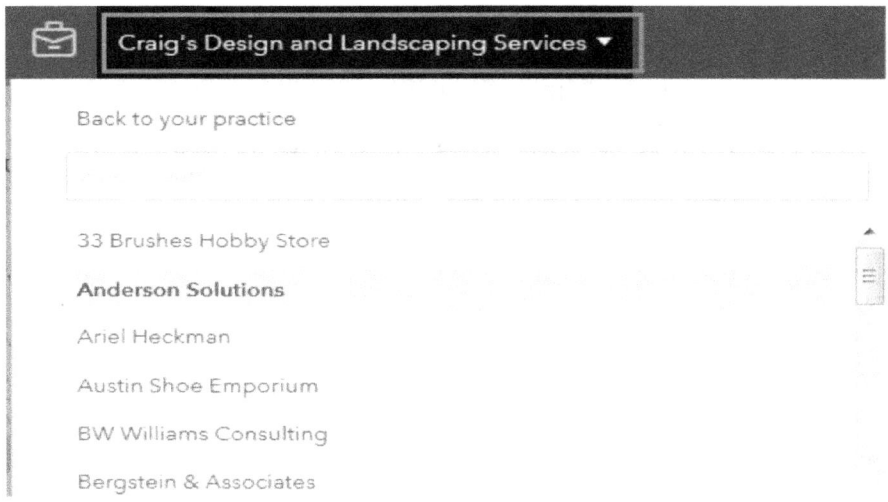

2. Configure the Settings

Under the Gear Menu, you'll discover the Account and Settings. This is the place you and your customers can configure their QuickBooks Online to fit the necessities of their organization best.

Once inside the Account and Settings segment, I recommend all accountant users get acquainted with the advanced tab. Here, you'll discover choices, for example, close the Books (where you can set an end date and password) and Enable Account Numbers.

Note: The Billing and Subscription tab will possibly show up if your customer is paying for their membership. If you are utilizing Wholesale Billing, you'll deal with the customer's charging and membership through QuickBooks Online Accountant.

3. Set up the Chart of Accounts

An incredible Chart of Accounts is critical to strong reporting. You can get to yours from the rigging symbol menu, the Accounting tab on the left board, or your Accountant toolbox. You can set up the Chart of Accounts physically or by bringing in a current rundown from Excel. If you've changed over a customer's QuickBooks Desktop record, the Chart of Accounts changes over also.

Click the pencil symbol in the upper right to assign or alter account numbers/names in a bunch as opposed to altering every one exclusively.

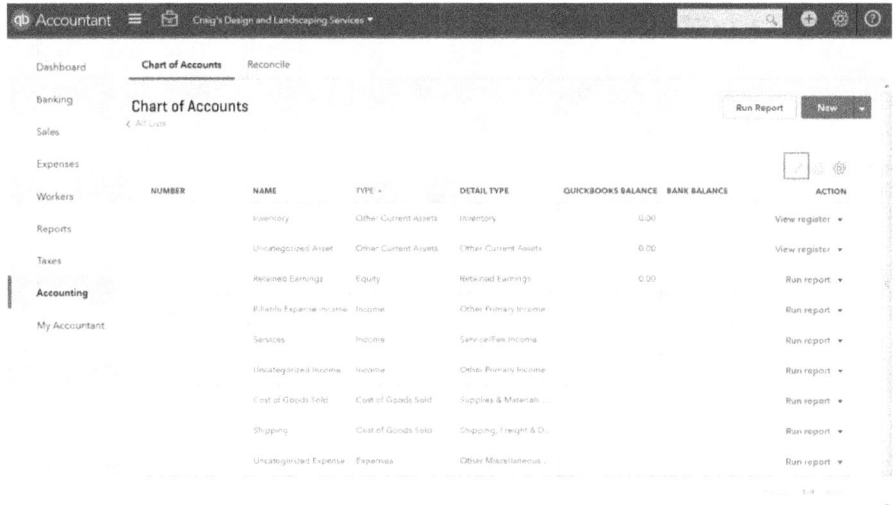

The drop-down menus under the Action section on the extreme right give the alternative to alter accounts exclusively, erase records or mark them inactive.

4. Associate Bank and Credit Card Accounts

If you haven't yet, work with your customers to associate with their financial organizations, which will help you both save time and decrease information passage. You can do this in the Banking tab in the left nav.

When records are associated, you can survey, order, and acknowledge exchanges from the bank into QuickBooks. QuickBooks Online has worked in auto-categorization that gains from you after some time. You additionally have the choice to match to existing exchanges recorded in the register.

Toggle over to the Bank Rules tab along the top to refine how QuickBooks Online classifies exchanges. This is particularly useful for customers who are uncertain how to sort exchanges themselves or have a high volume of comparable exchanges. Note: Check out my ongoing arrangement on bank feeds.

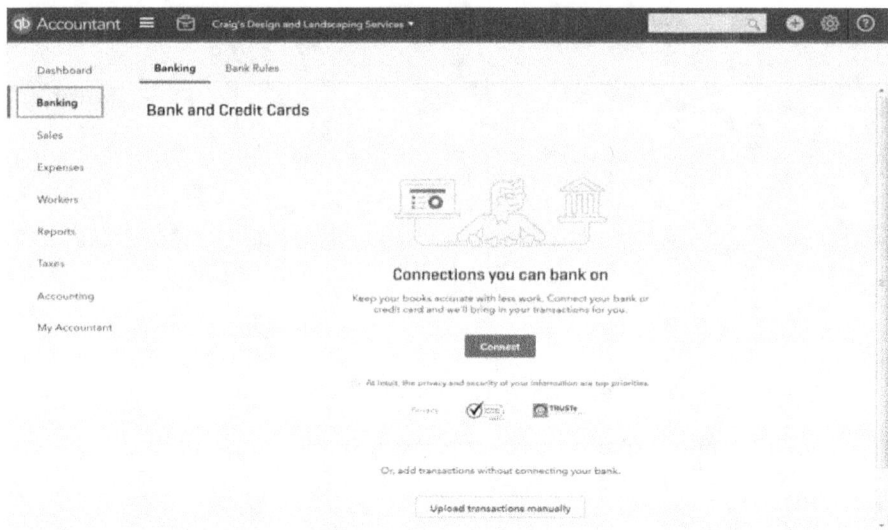

5. Make Transactions Recurring

If your customer is utilizing QuickBooks Online Essentials or Plus, you'll have a choice to make numerous kinds of transactions recurring. You can set these up under the gear-icon menu. Automating transactions assists spare with timing and improve accuracy, particularly when utilized with the bank feed.

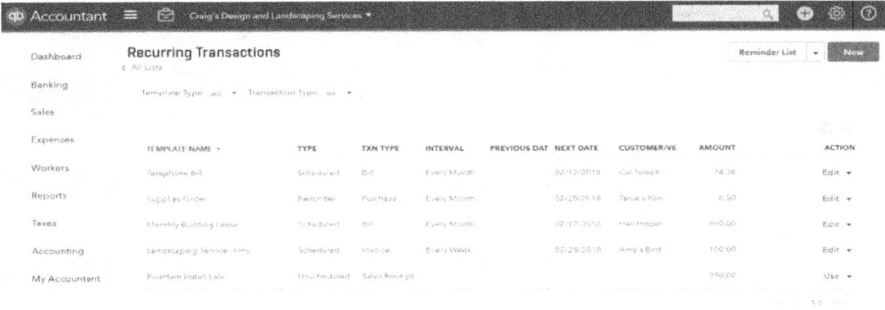

You can schedule transactions to happen automatically, set up updates, and make unscheduled templates.

6. Build a My Custom Reports List

Explore to the Reports tab to open the rundown of reports remembered for your customer's membership. You can design most reports in QuickBooks Online to meet best your and your customer's requirements and spare reports you customize for later use. You'll get to your My Custom Reports list from the accountant toolbox.

We surface a few as often as possible utilized alternatives along the highest point of each report to make it simpler to customize quickly, for example, picking your report period or exchanging between money/gathering basis. Continuously click Run report to mirror your changes.

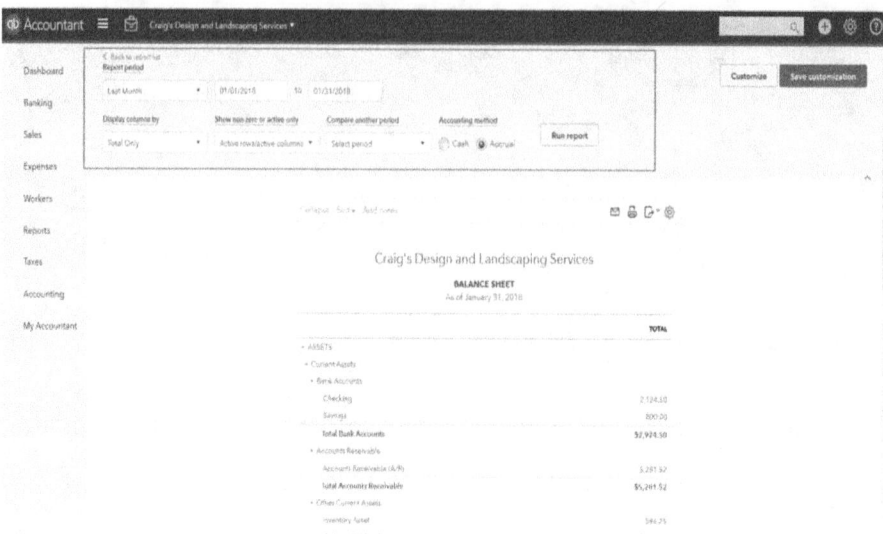

Click Customize in the upper right to see the full alternatives for the report. The customization choices will differ dependent on the report you run.

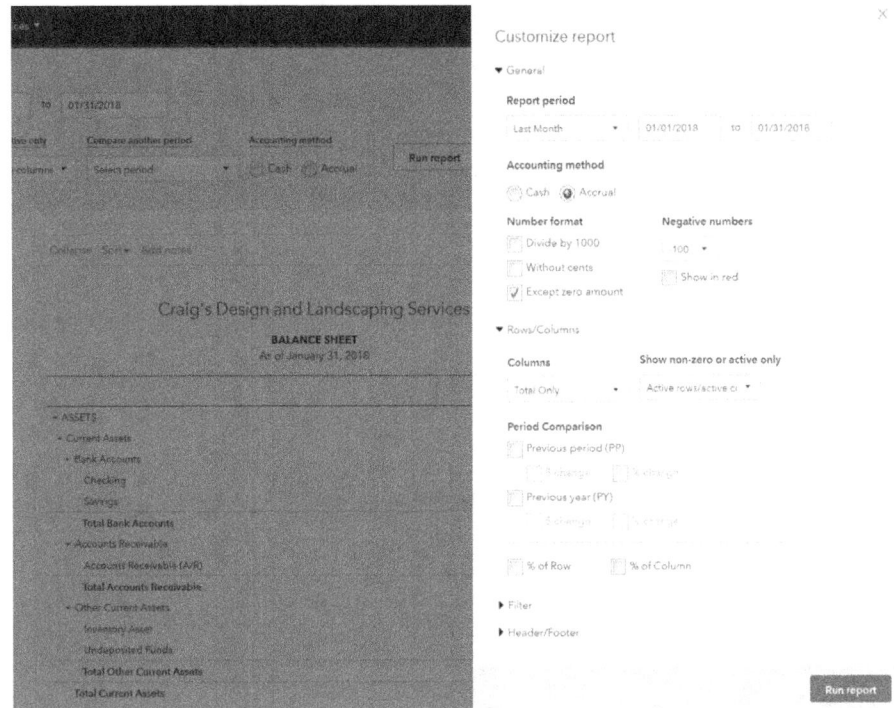

When your preferences are set, click save customizations to add the report to your My Custom Reports list. When saving, you'll have alternatives to give your custom report a name, add it to a gathering whenever wanted, and decide to share will all clients or just your firm.

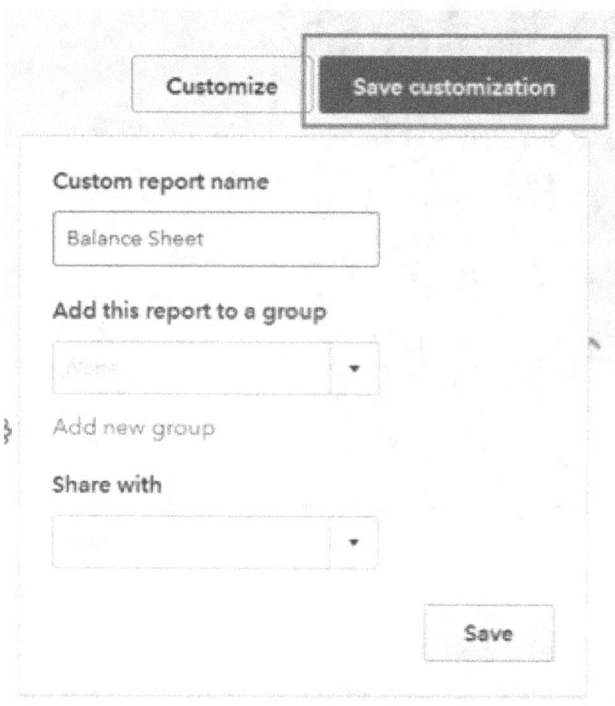

In the My Custom Reports show, you can run your reports, fare to PDF, change your sharing settings, and view reports others have shared with you.

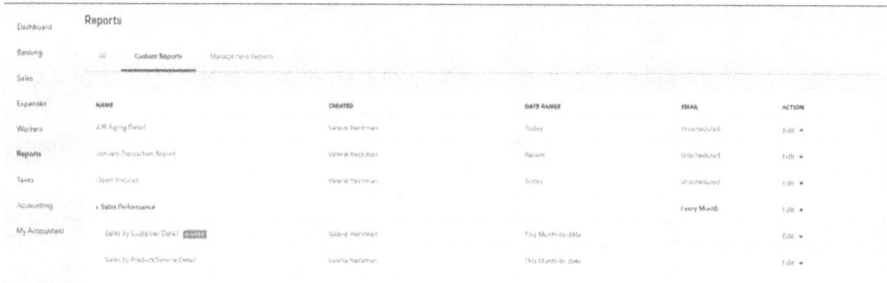

Also, you can plan a single report or gathering of reports to email naturally on a recurring schedule.

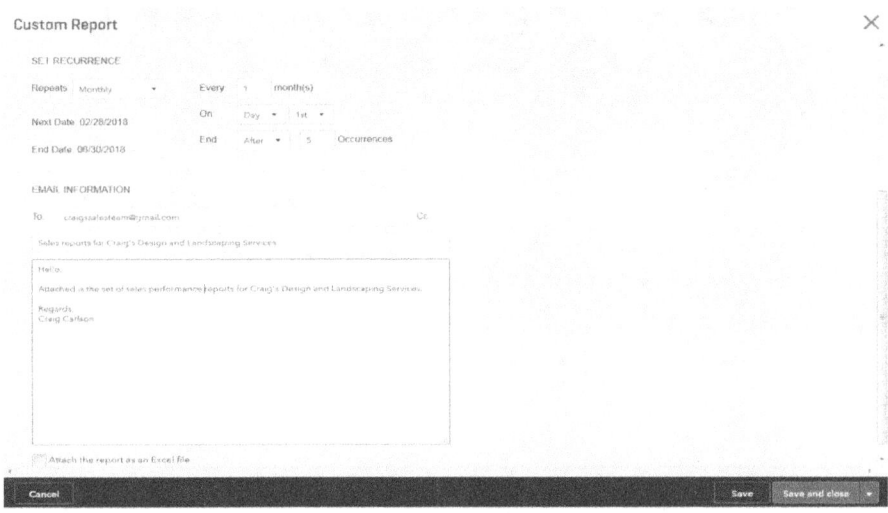

7. View Windows Side-by-Side

Utilizing program tabs, you can open different windows in QuickBooks Online simultaneously. This makes it simple to analyze, cross-reference, or perform multiple tasks without shutting the page you are working on.

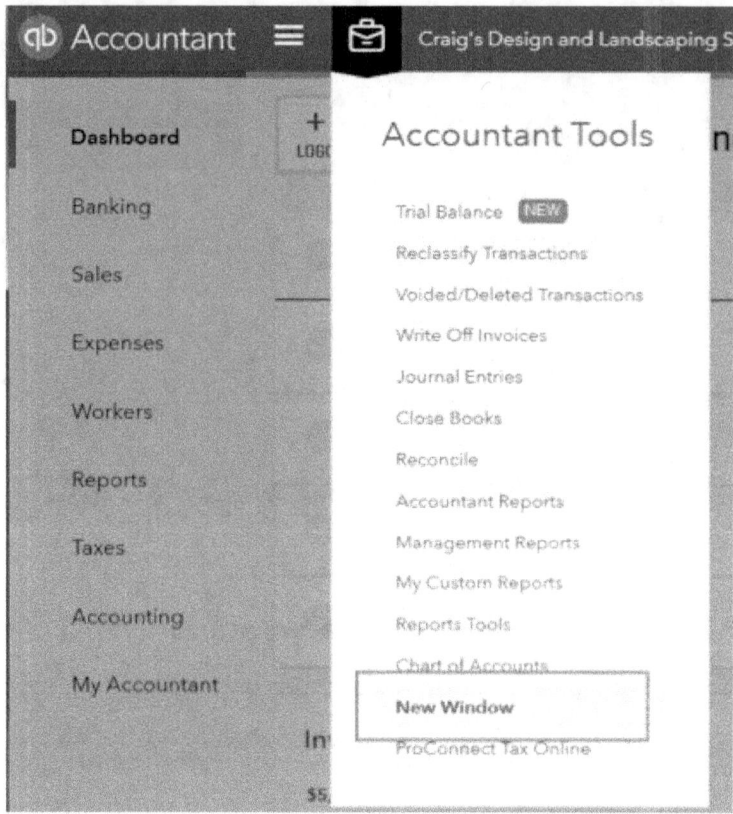

Accountants additionally have an easy route under the accountant tool kit called New Window, which will copy your present page in another tab.

In many programs, you can also right-click a tab and left-click Duplicate.

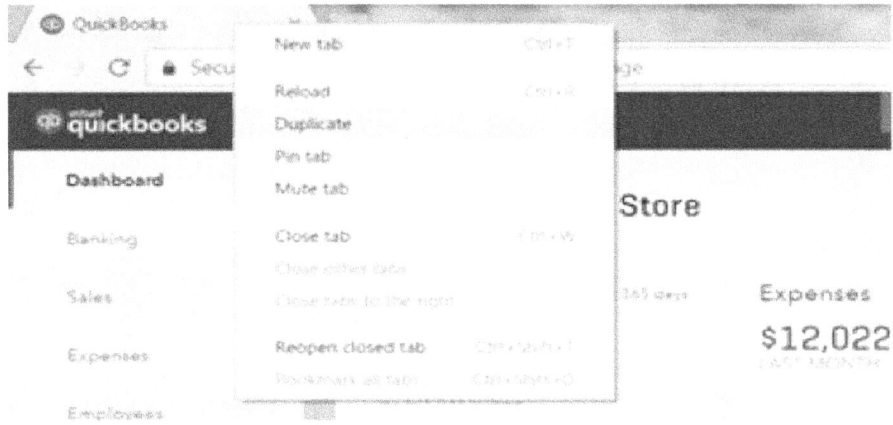

You can open the same number of tabs as required and drag and drop them over numerous screens.

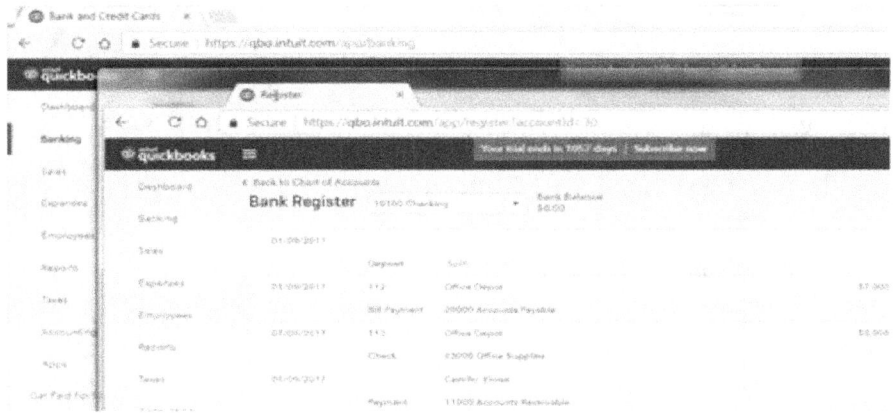

8. Survey the Audit Log

Under the apparatus symbol gear-icon menu, you'll discover the Audit Log. This log tracks increases and changes made to the organization's information and different exercises. It additionally monitors who signs in to the organization.

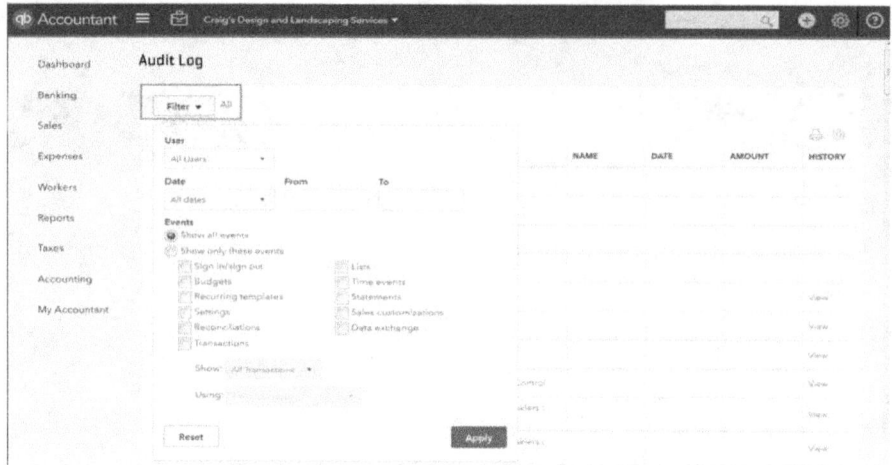

The review log can't be crippled nor activities deleted. You can channel by client, date, and movement, and effectively look at changes after some time.

Note: When your customer sees the review log, we don't show any client details, just the name of your firm.

9. Explore the Accountant Toolbox

As referenced, accountants have a spot to discover instruments that are select to accountants, just as alternate ways to the tools and exchanges, we think you'll utilize most.

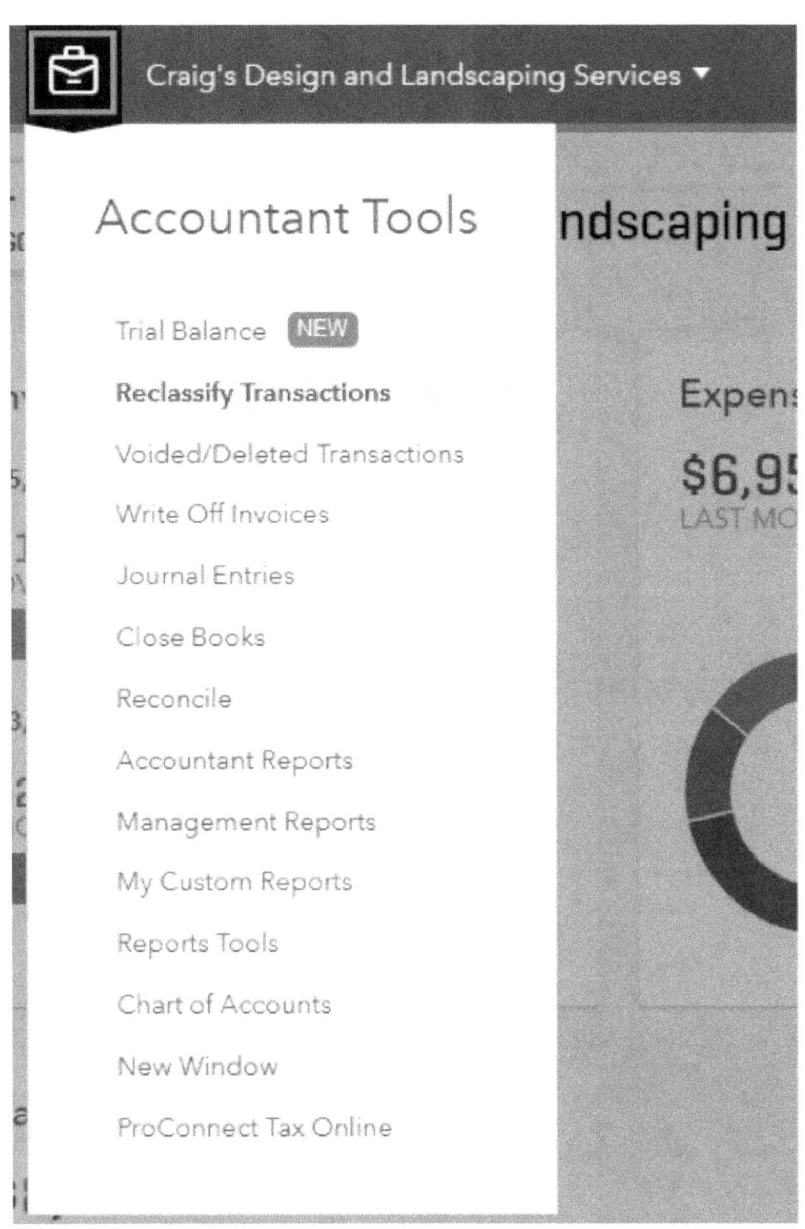

Here are a couple of accountant's just tools you should know:

Trial Balance empowers you to audit and modify the books in anticipation of a government form, without having to bounce between different applications. You can also map accounts and make, view, and document a government form in Intuit® ProConnect™ Tax Online.

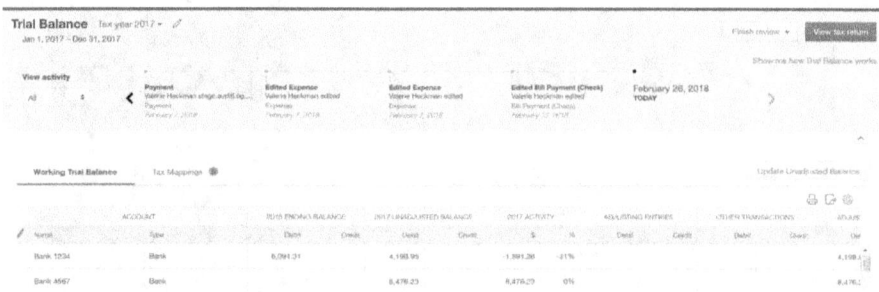

Rename Transactions can be utilized to make group changes to the class as well as record on numerous kinds of exchanges.

Reports Tools enables you to set a default date range and reason for different money related reports and other accountant devices.

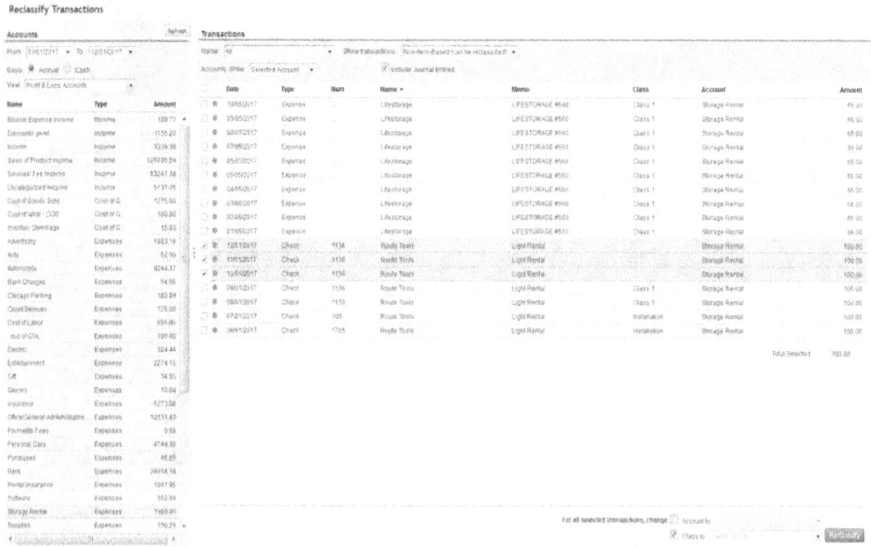

Bookkeepers additionally have the choice to check a diary passage as modifying and fix a reconciliation.

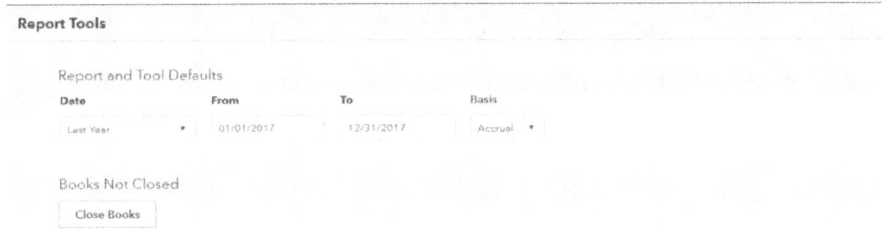

10. Get certified (and watch your firm develop!)

There's no better method to proceed with your QuickBooks Online instruction than by exploiting our free ProAdvisor® Program inside QuickBooks Online Accountant.

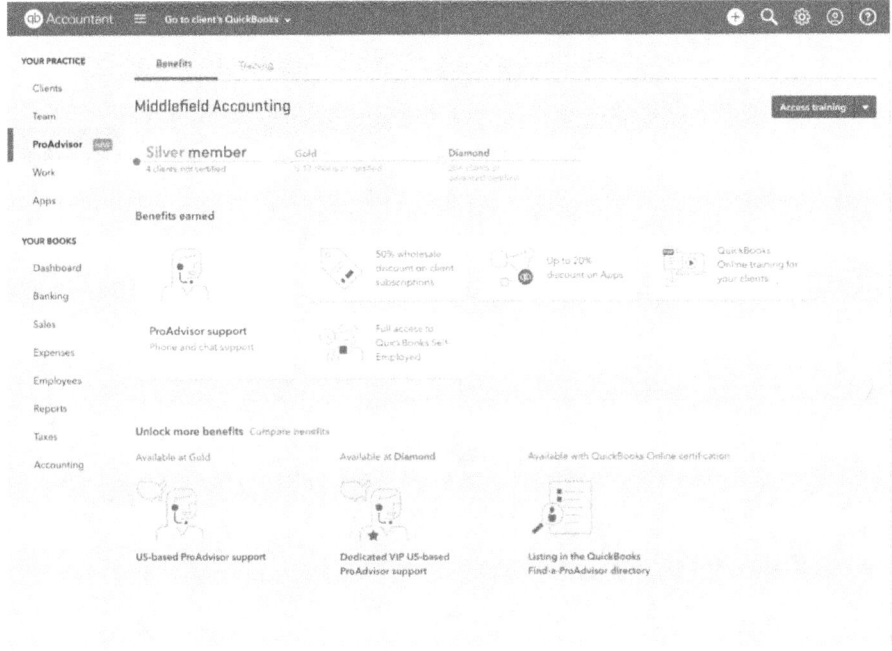

Take the QuickBooks Online Certification courses under the Training tab to extend your expertise (and win CPE!). At the point when you pass through the certification test, you'll have unlimited U.S. - based proAdvisor telephone support and the choice to list your profile on the Find-A-ProAdvisor online index, making it simple for new customers to find you.

QuickBooks Online Advanced Payroll - Getting started.

Utilizing standard QuickBooks Online Payroll? See Turn on and set up payroll.

Follow this manual to complete your finance arrangement rapidly and precisely

Required documents

Having the below data convenient will make the arrangement procedure simpler:

1. Your payroll registration sees from the Canada Revenue Agency (CRA), which has significant organization data like your legitimate name, place of work, and CRA finance account number. You'll also require the letter from the CRA showing your remittance frequency.
2. A check from your business financial balance or another record that contains all the financial details required to finish your bank arrangement.
3. Any documents you've gotten from commonplace expense organizations or worksheets, for example, your Workers' pay account details or pertinent commonplace assessments, similar to the Employer Health Tax in Ontario

4. Your workers' government and common TD1 forms with all significant individual subtleties, for example, complete name, birth date, and Social Insurance Number (SIN), finished.
5. A duplicate of voided checks from every one of your workers or contractors to set up the direct store

In case you're exchanging payroll suppliers, you ought to also produce a report of all worker compensation, and expenses paid, just as the sums for any business charges. This data should be gone into QuickBooks Online Advanced Payroll as a piece of the year-end reporting requirements.

Signup for QuickBooks Online Advanced Payroll

1. Open your QuickBooks Online record.
2. Navigate to the Employees tab.
3. Select Set up Payroll.
4. Select the features that issue to you to see an item correlation of our two finance contributions.
5. Use the price calculator to one side of the component outline to check your potential expense for QuickBooks Online Advanced Payroll.
6. Select free 30-days trial under the Advanced Payroll controlled by Wage point section.
7. Select Agree and connect.

Set up

- Once you've joined, you'll see a Setup finance screen with five segments to round out.
- Select Add to enter the data in each segment.
- You can also edit a segment before presenting the data. See down for details on what data is required for each area.

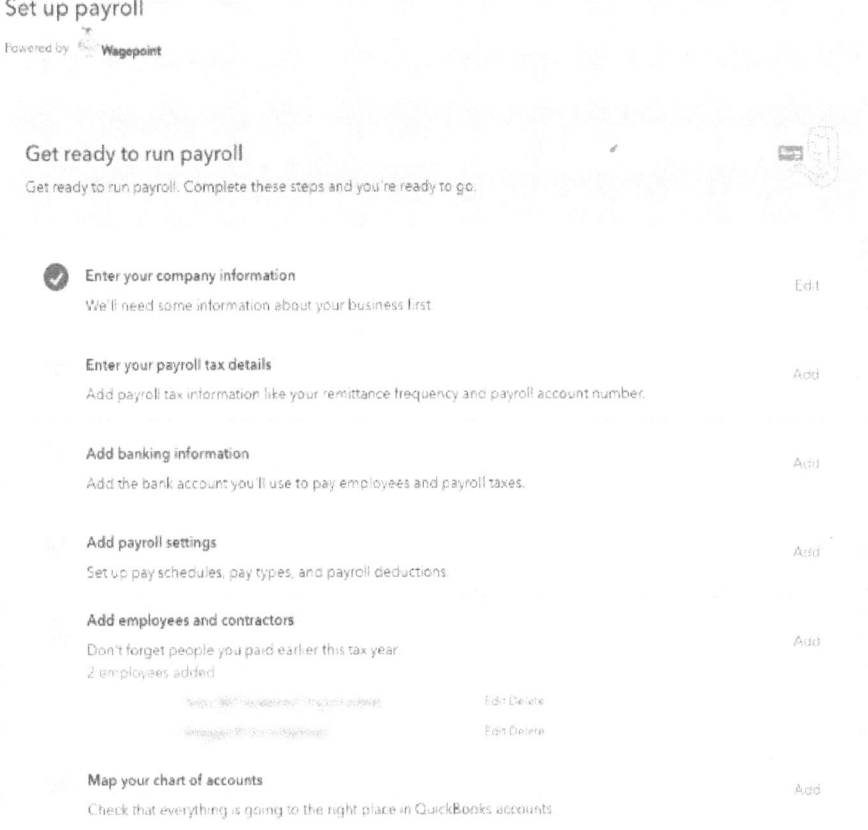

Enter your organization data

Disclose to us somewhat about your organization. We'll utilize this data on your payroll tax documents.

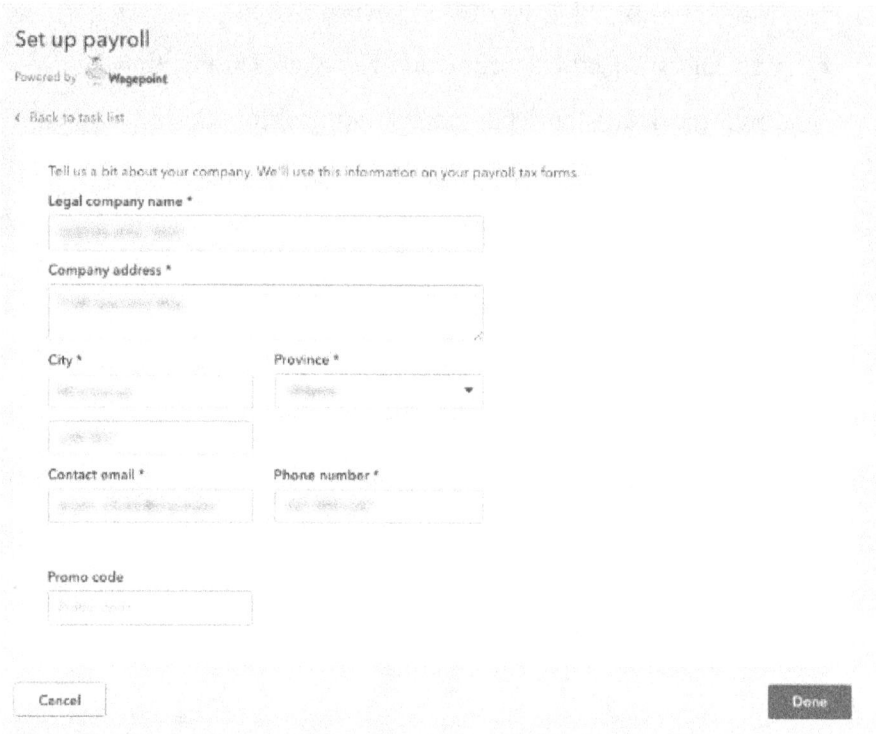

1. Legal organization name (The business name you use on government forms and authoritative records),
2. Company location, Email (We'll send you finance updates and notices)
3. Phone number (utilized for tax documents)
4. You can also enter a Promo Code if one was given.
5. When finished, select done.

Enter your payroll tax details

We deal with all-expense installments to the service for your benefit. If you might want to be responsible for making those installments yourself, you can turn off this feature. Quarterly remittances are not upheld as of now. If you are uncertain, kindly contact the CRA for more data.

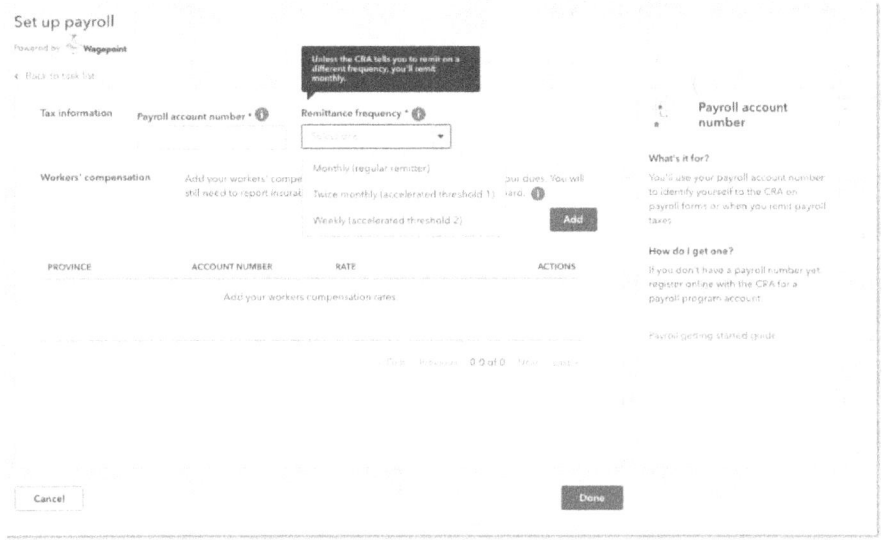

CRA Account number

- Payroll account number: Your 9-digit business number + RP + your 4-digit account number. (Like this: 123456789 RP0001)
- You'll utilize your payroll account number to recognize yourself to the CRA on finance forms or when you dispatch charges.
- Quebec finance account number: You're 10-digit Québec Enterprise Number (NEQ) + RS + your 4-digit account number. (Like this: 1234567890 RS0001)

- You'll utilize your Québec finance number to distinguish yourself from Revenue Québec on payroll forms or when you remit payroll charges.

Note: Please guarantee these numbers are exact to stay away from missed installments.

Remittance frequency

Your remittance frequency reveals to us how frequently you send the finance assessments to the CRA or Revenue Québec. This incorporates the expenses you pay and the duties you retain from workers' checks. If the CRA or Revenue Québec hasn't revealed to you how regularly to dispatch your taxes, select month to month. They'll fill you in regarding whether you have to begin transmitting all the more regularly, and you can change your recurrence in your finance settings whenever.

Frequency	Due Date
Monthly (Non-accelerated)	• 15th of the following month
Bi-weekly (Accelerated threshold 1)	• 25th of the month for remuneration that you pay or give from the 1st to the 15th of the month inclusive • 10th of the next month for remuneration that you pay or give from the 16th to the last day of the month
Weekly (Accelerated threshold 2)	Due on the 3rd working day after the end of the following: • From the 1st to the 7th day of the month, inclusive • From the 8th to the 14th day of the month, inclusive • From the 15th to the 21st day of the month, inclusive • From the 22nd to the last day of the month, inclusive

Note: If you pick in for this element, the charges will be pulled back from the financial balance on record when you run payroll, and held in trust and remitted for your sake as per the remittance frequency you picked during the setup. For more data on remittance frequencies, if it's not too much trouble, visit Canada.ca. QuickBooks Online Advanced Payroll naturally sets the payroll interval and pay dates after your first finance in the framework.

Workers' compensation

It covers lost wages, social insurance, and rehabilitation services for workers who are harmed at work, and protects you from claims from harmed laborers. If you enlist representatives or contractual workers, you likely need to pay into laborers' remuneration. Here you can include your rates so we can figure and transmit your duty. You will, at present, need to report insurable income to the laborers' compensation board. If you are uncertain what your WCB rate is if you don't mind looking at the Canadian Center for Occupational Health and Safety for more information.

To include a WCB rate, select Add rate and pick your:

- Province
- Account number (The number your commonplace Workers pay board gave you when you registered)
- Rate (Rate is given by the commonplace specialists' remuneration board
- At the point when finished, select done.

Note: You'll possibly observe a possibility for Revenue Quebec information if your central command is in Quebec, or you include a worker who works in Quebec.

Include banking data

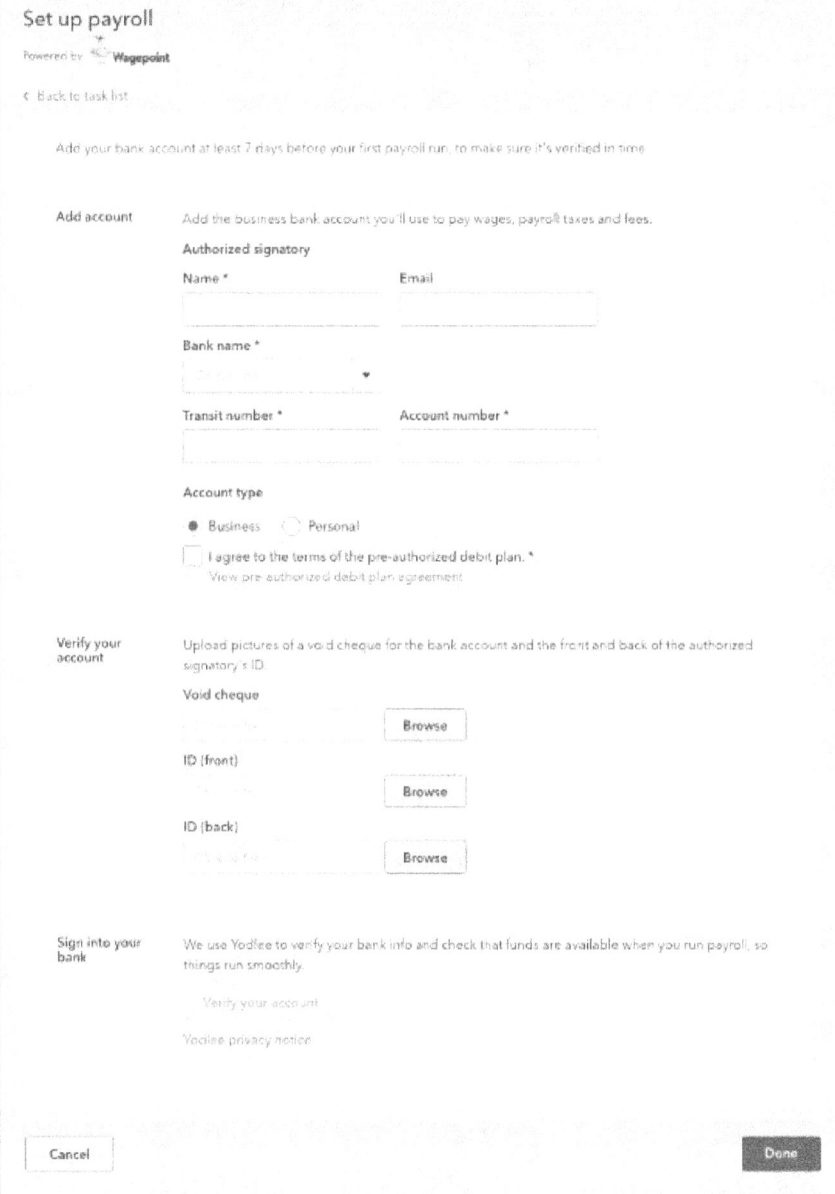

Significant: Please allow 2-4 business days after you have finished each of the three pieces of the ledger approval for your record to be confirmed and prepared to run payroll:

- Micro-deposit verification
- Cheque/ID transfer
- Yodlee check

Note: Direct store, Workers pay and source conclusions will be pulled back as a single amount, and show on your bank explanation as Intuit Trust Pay. You can see your invoices in the reports segment.

1. Add the Name and Email of the Authorized bank marking official for the bank account being utilized. The approved bank marking official or approved signatory ought to be set up as a Company admin with all entrance to the QBO account.
2. Select your Bank name starting from the drop list, and enter your Transit number and Account number
3. Choose the Account type (Business or Personal)
4. The Authorized marking official for the organization ought to consent to the terms of the Pre-approved charge plan understanding
5. Upload the necessary reports - void Cheque for the financial balance and government provided the personal ID of the approved marking official
6. Sign in to your internet banking account as the last confirmation step

7. When finished, select done
8. You won't have the option to finance until you complete the micro-deposit and Yodlee check. (2-4 business days after arrangement)
   a) Check your financial balance to get the test sum.
   b) Select the Gear symbol at the top, at that point Payroll settings
   c) Select Bank Account
   d) Enter the Amount of the test exchange in the field provided
   e) Select Complete approval
   f) Select Verify Account
   g) Choose to Get started in the spring up screen
   h) Search for or select your bank foundation from the list of choices
   i) Enter your web-based banking credentials. The web-based financial certifications are not put away or spared
   j) Select the ledger you set up in Advanced Payroll
   k) Select Confirm
9. The Risk and Compliance group audits the data accommodated your new financial balance (2 - 4 business days after setup is finished).
10. Once approved, the Run finance catch will be empowered

Note: Payroll should be handled three business days before the compensation date. This implies the vital finances should likewise be accessible in your financial balance three days preceding compensation day.

Add payroll settings

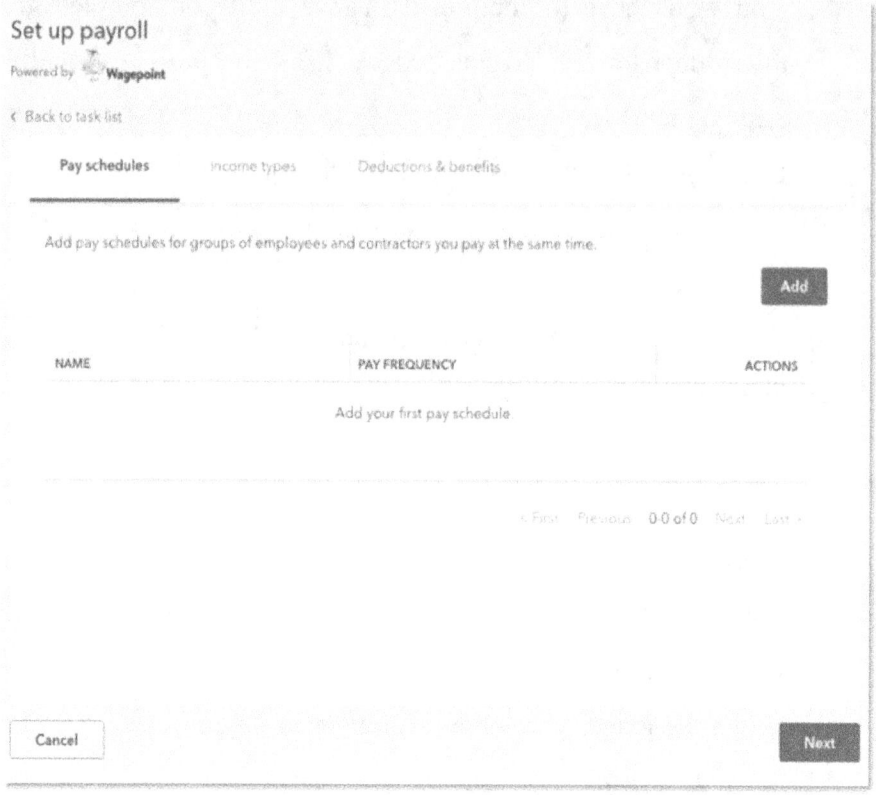

This segment has three tabs: Set up Pay gatherings, Income, and Deductions.

1. **Pay timetable -** Add workers and temporary workers to pay groups. To assist you with the beginning, we've naturally included some default groups.
   a. Select Add pay plan
   b. You can browse five frequencies: Weekly, Bi-week after week, Semi-month to month, Monthly, or Quarterly
   c. After picking a Frequency, you can Name it in the field provided

d. Select Done when finished

2. **Income sort** - Add the kinds of payment you pay to workers or temporary workers. We've begun you off with some regular ones. You can also demand another salary type if you don't perceive what you're searching for.

To include an income:

a. Select Add Income type
b. Choose from the Income type drop-down list. You can redo how this rundown will appear on pay stubs by entering an Income name in the space provided

If you look down, you will check whether the pay type chose Taxable, Payable, Pensionable, or Insurable. These are CRA standard settings, and you won't have the option to transform them

To request a custom income type:

a. Select Request custom salary
b. Enter the ideal Income type name
c. You can also choose what charges are appropriate (CPP/QPP, EI, Federal Tax, Provincial Tax, Health charge relevant and payable)
d. You can also pick which box (14/A, 40/L or Other) this salary will appear on the T4/Releve form
e. Enter any extra notes, and picked Send when finished

    f. You will get an email showing whether your request was added to the list

NOTE: You can include a reoccurring pay (reward, additional time, occasion, and excursion) to workers and temporary workers.

    3. **Deductions/Benefits** - Things like health advantages or RRSP commitments that you deduct from workers or temporary workers' compensation. You can also demand another reasoning kind if you don't see the one you're searching for.

To include another finding:

    a. Select Add derivation/advantage
    b. Choose from the Deduction/advantage type drop-down list. You can customize how this will appear on pay stubs by entering a Deduction/advantage name in the space provided
    c. If you look below, you will check whether the pay type chose Taxable, Pensionable, or Insurable. These are CRA standard settings, and you won't have the option to transform them

To demand a custom reasoning/advantage type:

    a. Select Request custom conclusion. You'll be incited with a book box to clarify the deduction request.
    b. Select Send when finished
    c. You'll get an email showing whether your solicitation was added to the list

d. When finished with this area, select Save or Back to the task list.

Add employees and contractors

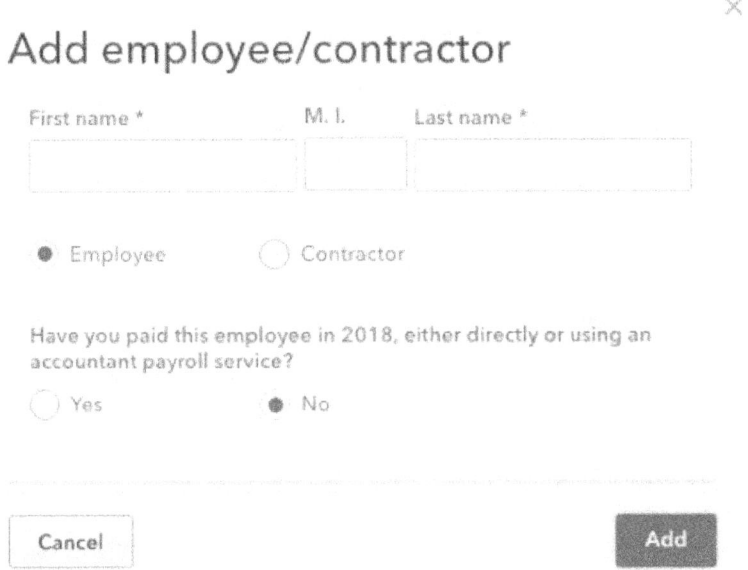

In this segment, you can include workers and temporary workers that you paid before this duty year.

1. When you click the Add button for this area, you'll see spring up a window that enables you to add somebody to your payroll
2. Enter their Name and Last name
3. Select whether they are an Employee or a Contractor
4. Choose Yes or No when asked, "Have you paid this representative in 2017, either straightforwardly or utilizing an accountant payroll service?"
5. Select Add when finished
6. You will currently observe a few tabs over the screen:

- **Profile:** Name, Social Insurance Number (SIN), Date of Birth (DOB), Hire date, Address, Email, Phone
- **Employment:** Compensation rate, Hours out of every week, Pay gathering, Departments, Locations, Job Titles, Workers' Compensation rate, Vacation strategy
- **Taxes:** Federal TD-1 sum, Additional retentions, Work area, Provincial TD1, Income Tax/CPP/EI Exempt
- **Direct Deposit:** Add Banking information for Employee's Direct Deposit - Deposit Priority, Bank, Transit Number, and Account Number. (This is utilized for service charges and direct store)
- **Income:** Income types, Amount, Frequency, Hours related
- **Deductions:** Deduction Type, Amount, Frequency, Employee commitment, Company Contribution

Significant: You should enter all representative's YTD payroll history before running payroll.

1. Enter the necessary data for every tab and select Save.

Map your chart of accounts

We made some default accounts for you to get things going. You should pick your Bank account. You can penetrate down under each area if you need to watch that everything is going to the correct spot in your QuickBooks Online records.

2. Choose your Bank Account starting from the drop list. This is the place we'll show the payroll charges that leave your bank account. You can also make another record from this screen.
3. Select the Advanced drop-down to see the top-level pre-chosen accounts.
4. You can choose the top-level record to see all the sub-accounts in it.
5. You can change any records you need and pick done when finished.

Set up payroll

Powered by ~~Wagepoint~~

‹ Back to task list

Check your Chart of Accounts

This is how we'll organize your payroll expenses and liabilities to you get a clear picture of your payroll costs. ⓘ

Payroll bank account *

This is where we'll show the payroll charges that come out of your bank account.

| Payroll bank account | Add new ▼ |

Advanced ︿

Payroll clearing account

After you run payroll, tax and direct deposit amounts show here until the pay run is processed.

| All payroll clearing accounts ∨ | Advanced Payroll ▼ |

Wages & earnings expenses

The expense for things like regular pay, overtime, and commission that you pay to employees & contractors.

| All wages & earnings expenses ∨ | Payroll Expenses W ▼ |

Employee benefits expenses

The expense for company contributions you pay into employee benefits like health plans or RRSPs.

| All employee benefits expenses ∨ | Payroll Expenses E ▼ |

Payroll tax expenses

The expense for the portion you pay for payroll taxes like CPP and EI.

| All payroll tax expenses ∨ | Payroll Expenses T ▼ |

Payroll tax liabilities

The amounts you deduct from employees & the portion you pay to CRA or Revenu Québec for payroll taxes.

| All payroll tax owed ∨ | Payroll taxes ▼ |

Benefits & deductions liabilities

The amounts you deduct from employees & the portion you pay for benefits like health plans and RRSPs.

| All benefits & deductions liabilities ∨ | Benefits & deducti ▼ |

Wages & earnings liabilities

The liability for things like regular pay, overtime, and commission that you pay to employees & contractors.

| Net pay - manual | Payroll Liabilities ▼ |
| Vacation pay accrued | ▼ |

Payroll subscription fees

The taxes and fees you pay for using Advanced Payroll.

| Processing fees expenses | Payroll processing ▼ |
| Sales tax expenses | Payroll processing ▼ |

Chart of Accounts

What is it?

This chart of accounts is a list of categories we use to keep track of what you have, owe, earn, and spend so you can see those details on reports. We map the payroll chart of accounts to QuickBooks so payroll transactions show up in your QuickBooks accounts and reports too.

What do I do here?

All you have to do is map your bank account—we took care of the rest. You can edit the account settings anytime to get more detailed reporting, but we recommend talking to an accountant first.

Payroll getting started guide

Cancel   Done

Updates:

- If you have the business charge focus turned on in QuickBooks Online, you will utilize the Sales charge on processing expenses.
- If the business charge focus isn't on, you will need to utilize Sales charge costs.
- If you're uncertain how to follow charges or credits, kindly consult an accountant.

1. To make changes after the arrangement:
2. Select the Gear symbol.
3. Choose Payroll settings.
4. Navigate to the Chart of the records tab.

You'll see two separate diary passages for each pay run.

Journal Entry 1

- Syncs to your QBO account on the day payroll is run
- Debits the clearing records and credits the financial balance.

Journal Entry 2

- Syncs to your QBO account on the compensation date
- Credits the clearing account charges costs and liabilities.

Create, edit, and manage budgets

QuickBooks Online Plus has an easy-to-navigate budgeting feature. Spending plans assist you with preparing so you can remain over your costs and income. After you set one up, utilize the Budget versus Actuals report to help settle on educated choices for your business.

Set the money related year's first month

Your spending begins with the primary month of your money related year, so it's a smart thought to confirm that the Financial Year setting is exact.

To confirm or change the financial year set:

1. Select Settings ⚙.
2. Select Account and Settings.
3. Select Advanced.
4. In the Accounting area, check that the setting in the first month of the financial year field is right, or select the pencil ✎ symbol to change the setting.
5. Select Save.
6. Select Done.

When you have confirmed that your money related year is right, the following stage is to survey the information you intend to put together your spending limit concerning guarantee that it's precise.

Review historical amounts

You can put together your spending limit concerning information either from the current money related year or from earlier year's amounts. If you intend to utilize historical information, it's a smart thought to run a Profit and Loss Detail report to ensure exchanges were assigned out accurately previously.

As a matter of course, the report shows exchanges made during the current monetary year to the present date, yet you can tweak the report to show the past money related year's amount.

1. To redo the Profit and Loss Detail report:
2. Select Reports.
3. Locate and open the Profit and Loss Detail report.

Select Last Financial Year (or Last Year if January is the primary month of your monetary year) from the Report time frame drop-down list to utilize the earlier year's information. To utilise information from the current financial year, acknowledge the default setting of This Year-to-date.

4. Select Run report.

The report shows information from the money related year you indicated. You can utilize this report to confirm that the exchanges you want to put together your financial limit concerning were effectively assigned.

Since you have confirmed the data to use in your spending limit, the subsequent stage is to make it.

Create your budget

You would now be able to make your budget limit. The Budgets highlight gives direction to assist you in making your first budget.

To create a budget:

1. Select Settings ⚙.
2. Under Tools, select Budgeting.
3. Select Add spending plan.
4. Enter a spending name in the Name field.
5. From the Financial Year drop-down list, select the money related year for the budget.
6. Use the alternatives on the Interval drop-down menu to indicate whether the budget is Monthly, Quarterly, or Yearly.
7. (Optional) From the Pre-fill information drop-down list, indicate whether to naturally enter information from the present or earlier year into the budget, and determine the year to utilize.
8. (Optional) From the Subdivide by drop-down list, determine whether to split the budget by Class, Customer, or Location, at that point, indicate what class, client, or area to add to the budget.
   - If you don't see Class or Location alternatives, those settings are not turned on. You can turn them on in the Categories segment of the advanced tab of Account and Settings accessible from the Gear ⚙ symbol on the toolbar.

9. Select Next.

10. If you didn't utilize the Pre-fill information alternatively, enter information into the table. Note: QuickBooks Online acknowledges decimals and doesn't adjust to the closest dollar. You can alter the sums whenever. On the off chance that you don't see every one of your records

and subaccounts, select the Gear ✿ symbol over the Total section and check whether the Hide clear columns alternative is chosen.

11. Select Save or Save and close.

Your budget is spared and recorded in the Budgets window.

Budget reports

You can see the following reports for the budget you made:

- Budget Overview: Summary of budgeted amounts for a particular specific budget.
- Budget versus Actuals: Summary of budgeted amounts versus actual amounts and their differences and fluctuation rates.

To see, email, print, or fare these reports:

1. Select Settings ✿.
2. Under Tools, select Budgeting.
3. Locate the monetary allowance to see, email, print, or export.
4. From the drop-down in the Action column, select Run Budget Overview report or Run Budget versus Actuals report.
5. On the Report page, select the Email or Print icon and, in the Print, email, or print as PDF dialogue, determine whether to make and send an Email with the budget report, or Print a duplicate of the financial limit. You can likewise save as PDF from this dialogue.

6. (Optional) Select the Export icon and select Export to Excel or Export to PDF, starting from the drop-down to send out the information in your budget. To see, email, print, or fare an alternate report, select a different budget plan from the Budget drop-down list.

Edit, copy or delete existing budget

At the point when you make another budget, existing spending reports are not overwritten or influenced.

To change a current plan, you should alter it each line in turn.

To edit a current spending plan:

1. Select Settings ✪.
2. Under Tools, select Budgeting.
3. Locate the budget to edit.
4. From the Action column drop-down menu, select Edit.
5. Edit the budget name or the budget amounts for every one of the comparing accounts, if important.
6. (Optional) For subdivided budgets, select one of the choices on the drop-down menu in the Show rows as the field to change the criteria the budget is subdivided by.
7. (Optional) Select the Gear ✪ icon over the Total segment and choose Month, Quarter, or Year under View by to change the budget interval.
8. Select Save or Save and close.
9. The budget is altered to reflect your updated data or settings.

To copy a budget

Copying a current spending plan enables you to make another spending utilizing your current budget amounts. This is extraordinarily useful if you need to utilize budget information for a past monetary year to make another one.

1. Select Settings ⚙.
2. Under Tools, select Budgeting.
3. Locate the budget to copy.
4. From the Action column drop-down menu, select Copy.
5. On the Copy Budget screen, enter the new spending name and financial year.
6. Select Create a Budget.
7. Update the budget amount as fundamental.
8. Select Save or Save and close.

The budget is copied with the name, year, and spending sums you determined.

To delete a current spending plan:

You can delete an existing budget, yet you should exercise when doing as such.

When a budget has been deleted, it can't be reestablished. The activity log holds a record of the deleted budget. However, it can't give any insights regarding it.

1. Select Settings ⚙.
2. Under Tools, select Budgeting.
3. From the Action column drop-down menu, select Delete.

The budget is presently totally deleted and can't be reestablished.

Financial Reports and Reporting Features

Reports show up on the Reports Tab Dashboard list (Reports Center), or you can scan for something explicit from the search field at the top. There are huge amounts of reports accessible. Most will pursue this titling show:

Some have quite certain utilization cases, giving you bunches of options. There are basic reports you'll need to run on every day or week after week premise, for example,

- Balance Sheet (which pursues the Balance Sheet Equation) – tracks assets, liabilities, and value of your business – what you "own" and "owe" inside a given timeframe.
- Assets - Make sure you comprehend the contrast between current assets (plan to sell inside one year) and fixed assets (huge purchases you intend to use throughout quite a while).
- Liabilities – once more, know the contrast between a present and long-term liabilities so you realize how to enter things like open bills and loans properly. Note that while liabilities are what you owe and you'd accept this should be a negative number, it's spoken to as a positive incentive here.

- Equity – the value of your business from the viewpoint of the owner (counting their commitments, owner's draw, and overall gain [activity from income and cost accounts]).
- Profit and Loss Statement - tracks your income and thinks about it against the cost of maintaining your business (for example, costs).

This is the most widely recognized report you're probably going to run. It's an outline of your pay and costs so you can see your cash flows.

Net Income is your profit after your total income, costs, and Cost of Goods Sold have been calculated. This line appears at the base of your Balance Sheet under Equity (above).

Sales by Product/Service Report – the simplest method to follow your deals that can be tweaked to show differing levels of detail.

There are three primary kinds of reports, and each has its uses.

Summary Reports – for pulling "overview" information with some applied investigation, which is the thing that you will likely utilize regularly or regularly.

- List reports – for pulling ", for example, all your current records or items and services.
- Detail reports – for pulling "by-line" datasets inside a predefined date go, for example, taking a look at your deals by the client.

Summary Reports center in around explicit data focuses, (for example, you're A/P or A/R or complete salary by accounts) without getting excessively lost in the line-by-line subtleties. Rather, get a mid-ranged outline of your records.

Craig's Design and Landscaping Services
PROFIT AND LOSS
January 1 - June 19, 2018

	TOTAL
▼ Income	
Design income	2,250.00
Discounts given	-89.50
▼ Landscaping Services	1,477.50
▼ Job Materials	
Fountains and Garden Lighting	2,246.50
Plants and Soil	2,351.97
Sprinklers and Drip Systems	138.00
Total Job Materials	4,736.47
▼ Labor	
Installation	250.00
Maintenance and Repair	50.00
Total Labor	300.00
Total Landscaping Services	6,513.97
Pest Control Services	110.00
Sales of Product Income	912.75
Services	503.55
Total Income	**$10,200.77**
▼ Cost of Goods Sold	
Cost of Goods Sold	405.00

These give account outlines just as individual line-by-line exchange details. "Client Balance Detail" and "Deals by Customer Detail" Reports are normal and helpful for focusing in on extremely limited data or recognizing a particular set of transactions.

[Profit and Loss Detail report for Craig's Design and Landscaping Services, January 1 – June 19, 2018]

The "group" work is also an incredible method to distinguish patterns while having particular details showed one next to the other in agreement.

List Reports help take a look at everything in your QuickBooks framework, from Products and Services to Employee data to Payment Methods utilized by your organization. Most are expansive, yet some can get genuinely tight, need to see every one of the bills you've paid in QuickBooks in the course of the most recent three months? There's a report for that.

Need to hand your group a list of contact messages; however, not their telephone numbers? Run a Customer List Report and alter it with the telephone number column removed.

Another utilization for List Reports is to clean up your information. Suppose you need to expel inert clients from your books however you have an enormous deals group: pull a CSV for (or print) a Customer List Report, sharing around your group to recognize who is no longer a client and hand it back to a single team member to make those clients latent.

Running custom reports in QuickBooks gives you a chance to limit in on the information that issues, render the information in manners that sound good to you, and eliminate extraneous details so you can undoubtedly focus on account points of interest. Also, going limited with reports implies to find out about how each piece of your business impacts its general wellbeing, which at last causes you settle on increasingly educated money related choices.

Custom reports offer a great deal of adaptability: you can apply different channels, arranging devices, and reaches to pull very specific data sets. Moreover, some custom reports need not be complicated, a Profit and Loss Report booked to be run and messaged on a Monthly premise is a basic one with incredible bits of knowledge about the direction of your business.

You can apply these customizations at the highest point of the structure in these two regions:

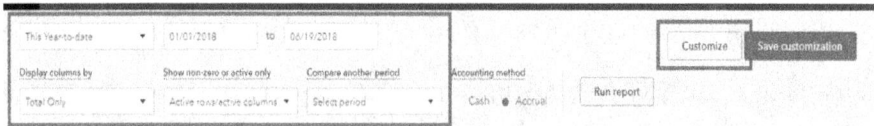

Contingent upon the report you use, diverse customization choices will be accessible, not all reports have similar arrangements of channels, and however, most do. Remember to hit "Run Report" to apply your customizations. Modifying also empowers some other cool features which we will go into later in the article.

Customizing reports with "channels" brings you to the cold earth from a high-elevation perspective on your business. Clicking "Customize" from either the report page or the vertical circle's tools by the report on the rundown gives you access to various channels for both line and segment report information.

Instead of browsing at the massively assorted cluster of customizations available to assemble a report, ask yourself, "what information am I truly interested in?" she that response to locate the fundamental channels to arrive at your answer - through this procedure you, will realize what is accessible.

Customizing reports by including evacuating or reordering segments is another incredible to render the information in manners that sound good to you and taking out data that isn't as helpful or potentially diverting, getting you to the experiences you need most with minimal measure of contact.

Showing figures as rates, as opposed to crude figures, is only one convincing motivation to dive into the revealing features.

When you locate the ideal set customizations, as opposed to returning a similar set each time you need this information, you can spare customization. Give spared reports an extraordinary name to recognize them and snap "spare customization" at the highest point of the report page.

Here are a couple of custom reports you should make and have available consistently:

Monthly Balance Sheet

Channels applied: ("All Dates," "Date-you-opened" to "1/1/2020," Display segments by "Months")

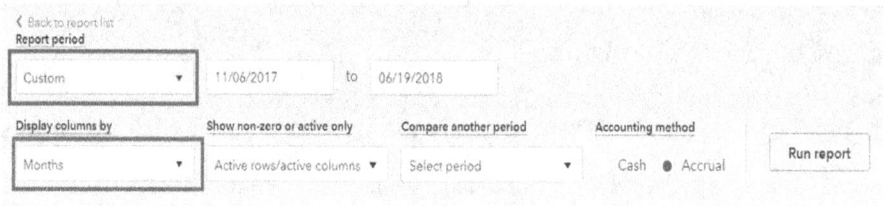

- Sales by Customer Detail Report for a high-esteem client John Freeman

Channels applied: ("All Dates," Customize - Filter "Client - by "Freeman Sporting Goods")

Customize report

▼ General

Report period

[All Dates ▼]

Accounting method

Cash ● Accrual

Number format

☐ Divide by 1000
☐ Without cents
☑ Except zero amount

Negative numbers

[-100 ▼]

☐ Show in red

▶ Rows/Columns

▼ Filter

☑ **Customer** [Freeman Sporting Go ▼]

☐ Distribution Account [All ▼]

☐ Vendor [All ▼]

☐ Employee [All ▼]

☐ Product/Service [All ▼]

▶ Header/Footer

Run report

- Profit and Loss Report for just Landscaping Installation Income (Service)

Channels applied: ("All Dates" Display sections by "Months," Customize – Filter Products/Service "Finishing Installation")

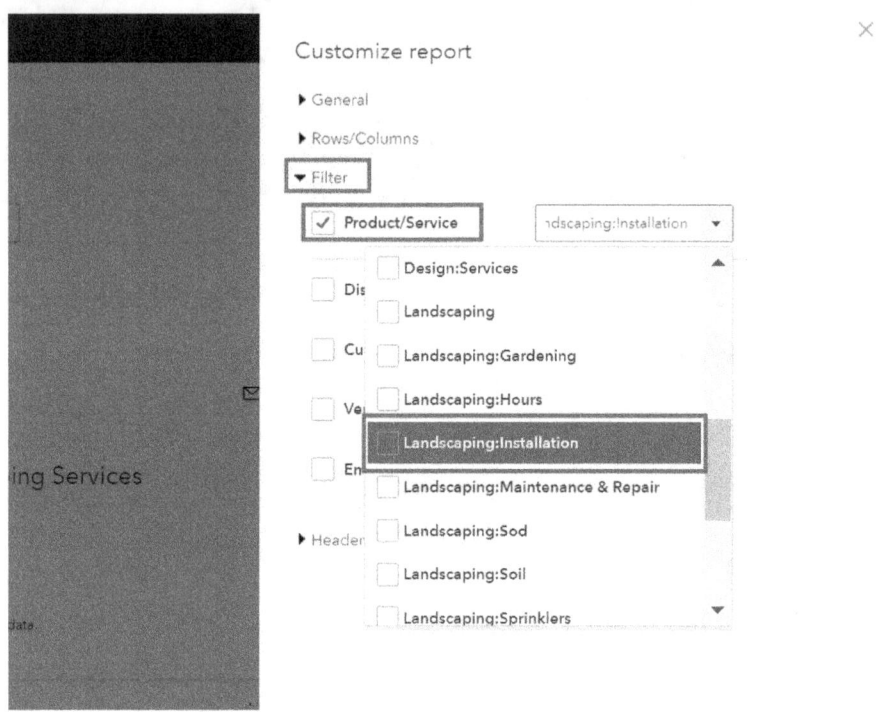

- Profit and Loss Report for week by week utility costs

Channels applied P and L report: ("All Dates," Display sections by "week" – Customize – Filters Distribution Account "Gas and Electric" and "Phone")

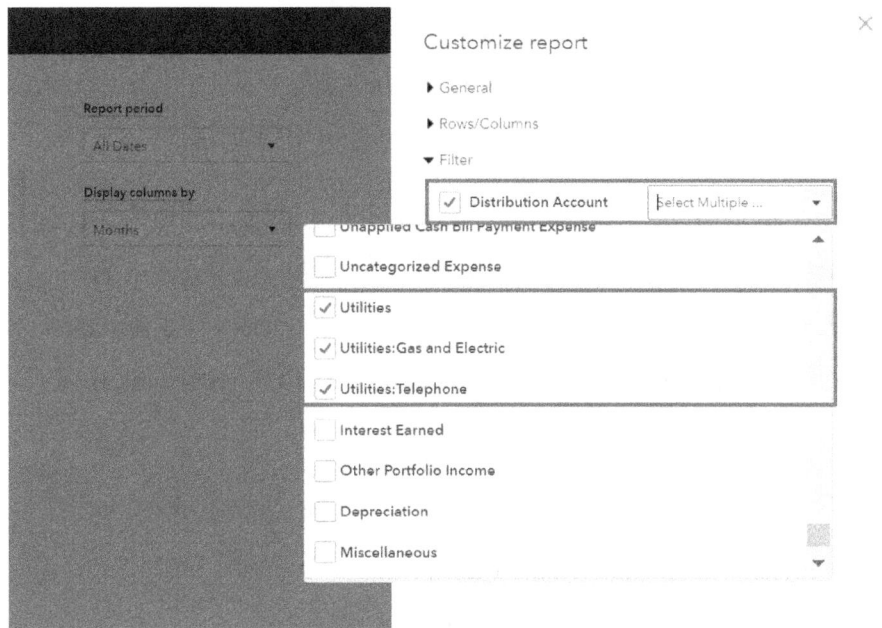

Saving reports additionally enables you to bunch them so you can set consent for who can access and view the information, which may be significant in case you're working with touchy data over a wide group.

Recollect too that reports consequently update with new information each time you run them.

The more features you can set on auto, the additional time you should concentrate on increasingly significant business matters.

There are recurrent reports you can plan immediately that concur with money related periods, for example, a month to month Profit and Loss Report or a week by week

Balance Sheet. Keep in mind, custom reports don't need to be unpredictable, and the interval might be sufficient to put it on this "repeating" email premise.

If there are custom reports you run routinely, or you need consistent reports on a specific report, think about booking them. From the start, plan them to send more regularly than you'd suspect you require and change from that point, it's smarter to stretch out beyond time than too little data past the point of no return.

To email reports, click on the Reports Tab and afterward the "Custom Reports" sub-tab. Select the report you need to alter, click "edit" and you can empower consents for the report – which is discrete from who will get the email. When you turn on a "set email plan," you can assign the date, time interval, and even set an end-date (or "none" for uncertain sending).

How to Use QuickBooks Efficiently

QuickBooks bookkeeping programming is a dependable tool that can simplify monitoring your business accounts. From invoicing and charging to accounting and following costs, to duties and installments, you currently have a progressively effective approach to keeping up your records.

We have arranged a couple of supportive tips on the most proficient method to utilize QuickBooks all the more adequately. These tips are also shown in the video below.

1. Pick a QuickBooks Version

QuickBooks has various versions of the product relying upon the necessities of your business. For instance, if you are a beginning business person, QuickBooks Simple Start is more appropriate for you than QuickBooks Enterprise, intended for bigger organizations with higher usefulness and stock control. For lower overheads, there is a QuickBooks Online alternative. What's more, recollect: you can generally redesign the product later, as your business advances, or use QuickBooks additional items.

2. Take advantage of the Preferences

The set-up wizard doesn't show every one of the features that you could be exploiting. By clicking (Edit – > Preferences), you can change your settings. For instance, you can mirror your organization's inclinations on the utilization of stock and requests, set default represents checks and bills, or decide to take advantage of the finance and expense features. You can also make the product progressively advantageous to use by including simple alters, like permitting the programmed position of decimal focuses on the numbers (Edit/Preferences/General/My Preferences).

3. Use the Navigation

QuickBooks works superbly at making the product basic and simple to utilize. Take advantage that by recalling simple, alternate routes: for example, use Ctrl-I for a new receipt, Ctrl-E for altering exchanges, or Ctrl-M for a Memorize Transactions field. Ctrl-F can open a Find feature to push you to find exchanges effectively.

- Ctrl-I – Create a receipt
- Ctrl-E – Edit exchange
- Ctrl-F – Find exchange
- Ctrl-J – Open Customer Center
- Ctrl-M – Memorize exchange or report
- Ctrl-N – New receipt, bill, check, or rundown thing in setting
- Ctrl-Q – a fast report of exchanges for everything in a list
- Ctrl-T – Open retained exchange list
- Ctrl-W – Write new check/open a compose checks window
- Alt + F4 = exits the QuickBooks programming
- Alt + Down Arrow Key = shows list for a field

(Shortcut image)

Customizing your symbol bar by changing your default symbol settings can also make an advantageous easy route course: you can include, evacuate or adjust the symbols, including changing their request and appearance, to better suit your work needs (Click menu – > Customize Icon Bar – > Select the symbol – > roll out your improvements – > Delete/Change/Edit – > OK) Other route features, for example, right-click menus, can fill in as a helpful option in contrast to utilizing toolbar symbols and menus.

4. Remain Organized with QuickBooks Features

There are different features that can assist you with remaining composed of QuickBooks. For example, QuickBooks Reports. To capitalize on the element, it might be important to familiarize yourself with the sorts of reports accessible. For instance, benefit and misfortune report shows salary and cost over a given timeframe, while an asset report clarifies how much your organization is worth. To ensure you can alter the report to suit your needs before it is shown, you can pick turn on the Modify Report feature (Edit – > Preferences – > Reports and Graph alternative – > Prompt Me to Modify the Report).

QuickBooks additionally encourages you to follow benefit and loss by utilizing Classes, for example, Marketing, Building an, and so on. At the point when Classes work is on (Edit – > Preferences – > Accounting – > Company Preferences – > Use class following), you have a chance to run a Profit and Loss by the Class report, and check and fix the inconsistencies by segments.

Another advantageous element is Memorize Transactions: it enables you to mechanize and recollect your bills. All you'll need is to change the sum of the date, and it will be added to the correct record!

5. Utilize the Support Features

You have free Intuit support options accessible – ensure you exploit them! One of the choices is to utilize Forums (Help – > Live Community): the appropriate response you are searching for might as have now been up there. You could also look through the QuickBooks Knowledge Base got a glance through the now and again asked questions.

Also, recall: you can generally reinforce your information to the cloud. To be safe.

Bonus

Did you realize you can utilize a Quick Math Calculator, which makes tallying increasingly fun and simpler to get to? Snap inside the field, press "=" sign, and a smaller than usual tape will seem to assist you with playing out your figuring's. Press Esc to leave the QuickMath feature.

Regardless of whether you are an entrepreneur or a bookkeeper, you can take advantage of QuickBooks and use it to assist you with accounting. Furthermore, if you need to find out additional, look at our QuickBooks course at Ashton College.

Here are the best 23 QuickBooks easy routes and tips from the professionals:

1. Incorporate Your Digital Order-Taking Solution with QuickBooks

At the point when you're in debt, it's significant that you take a 360° perspective on your business and survey where you can make cuts, what's working for you and what isn't. In case you're a B2B deals organization, you should take a look at shortening your request to-money process. This can be accomplished by incorporating your computerized request taking arrangement with QuickBooks, so the entire procedure is robotized, coming about in expanded proficiency as well as in a decrease in authoritative expenses and fewer request blunders. Diminishing your expenses like this is an incredible initial step to handling your business obligation.

2. Enter Multiple Items with the Same Name and Account Type All at Once

Make your life simple in QuickBooks Online with bank sustains. Connection your bank to your QBO account. In case you're attempting to enter various things with a similar name and record type, you can do them at the same time. Sort by depiction and mark off the entirety of the comparative things. For example, Office Depot. Select all charges to Office Depot by verifying them. At that point, go to Batch Actions and starting from the drop, pick Modify Selected. At that point, select Vendor (Office Depot) and Account (Office Supplies, or whatever record you use for this kind of cost). Select Apply, and you will see the entirety of the exchanges have now been coded effectively. From that point, you can return to Batch Actions and select Accept Selected.

3. Save Time by Creating a Custom Report

If you run a similar report routinely, you can save customized reports by picking your favored channels, renaming the custom report, and saving it. Whenever you need to run the report, all you ought to do is pick your new custom report from your rundown, and it will apply the channels you have saved. To make a custom report, go to the reports list in QuickBooks and pick the report you need to customize. At the point when the report opens, pick "customize" to change the information, channels, lines, sections, and so forth., click "run a report," and "spare customization." You can add the report to a gathering you have made, and you can even impart to others in your organization.

4. Utilize Attachments

Having the option to append records is perhaps the best element of QuickBooks. For instance, you can join a record like a lease agreement, agreement, or a resale testament to a client's detail page. You can likewise transfer your bank and financial records to the connections organizer so you or potentially your accountant can easily access them at whatever point essential.

5. Change Default Email Text Settings for Invoices, Pay Stubs, Statements

Inside the preferences of the QuickBooks organization document, change the default email content for invoices, pay stubs, statements, etc. For instance, for payroll and messaging the compensation stub to employees, you can change the layout message that workers get in their encrypted document. Change the default content from "your compensation stub is attached" to "your connected paystub is password ensured. Your password is the initial four letters of your last name and last four digits of your Social Security number." It will spare you time since you won't get the "what's my secret key to get to my compensation stub?" question over and over.

6. Set Up Bank Rules for Common Expenses

QuickBooks enables you to set up bank rules for basic costs like utility installments, normal vendors and providers, and others. If you don't have to audit installments made to water, power, and other normal costs each month, you can set up the bank rule to auto-add. This will save you a great deal of time.

7. Customize Your QuickBooks Icon Bar

You can customize your QuickBooks symbol bar by moving symbols around and changing the current ones to address your issues. You can evacuate a pointless symbol by setting off to the "view" menu and tapping on "customize symbol bar." Then pick and snap the symbol you need to erase. You can also pursue a similar procedure while including a symbol. Go to the "view" menu, click "customize icon bar," and pick a symbol from a rundown by clicking "Add" and "OK."

8. Invest Time to Learn QuickBooks Correctly

Invest some an opportunity to figure out how to utilize QuickBooks accurately. Frequently, entrepreneurs' books are disorganized because they chose to "make things up along the way" when it came to entering their pay and costs in QuickBooks. QuickBooks is a non-bookkeeper's product; you needn't bother with a bookkeeping degree to utilize it.

9. Be Consistent in How You Classify Your Expenses

While entrepreneurs have caution by the way they need to group certain costs, it's critical to make a standard for how they will be arranged and stick to it. If you change how you arrange your costs each quarter, your financial statements will show uncommon variances and inconsistencies that could adversely affect choices by banks and investors. Set up rules for how costs will be ordered and guarantee that anybody in your group utilizing QuickBooks follows these standards for steady data.

10. Utilize the QuickBooks Audit Trail to Protect Against Risk

The QuickBooks Audit Trail is significant. It rapidly bolds and stresses any exchange that has been controlled or changed. If more customers are utilizing the Audit Trail report as a major aspect of their continuous month to month survey and the board of their organization, they would almost certainly reveal extortion all the more rapidly, constraining the enthusiastic and money related effect to their association.

In what capacity can QuickBooks Self-Employed assist me with dealing with my taxes and forms?

Discover how QuickBooks Self-Employed can help you in dealing with your taxes and forms.

We've gathered together the most regularly asked questions concerning assessments and structures in QuickBooks Self-Employed. Here are some of them.

Would I be able to record my assessments with QuickBooks Self-Employed?

While QuickBooks Self-Employed encourages you to present your Quarterly Tax Payments, it doesn't deal with recording your annual tax return. Our tax bundle incorporates TurboTax Self-Employed, which you can use to get ready and document your yearly government form.

How does QuickBooks Self-Employed assist me with my Quarterly Taxes?

QuickBooks Self-Employed appraisals your Quarterly Estimated Taxes through the data from your Tax Profile, followed pay, costs, findings, and the projections for the rest of the year.

How would I utilize my QuickBooks information for charge time?

Audit and guarantee that all your data is prepared to document with QuickBooks Self-Employed Tax Checklist.

How would I run my year-end reports?

To guarantee you don't miss a significant conclusion, different payroll costs, run financial reports completing your Tax Checklist. The most significant reports for your tax file are the Tax Summary, Tax Details, Receipts, and Mileage Log.

Download Mileage log, Profit and misfortune, Receipts, Tax outline, and Tax details reports

1. In QuickBooks Self-Employed, go to Reports.
2. Download the Tax Summary report for 2018, the Tax Details report for 2018, and the Receipts report for 2018.

Download the Mileage Log

1. In QuickBooks Self-Employed, go to Miles.
2. Change the dating channel to 2018.
3. Select the Email or Export to Excel alternative.

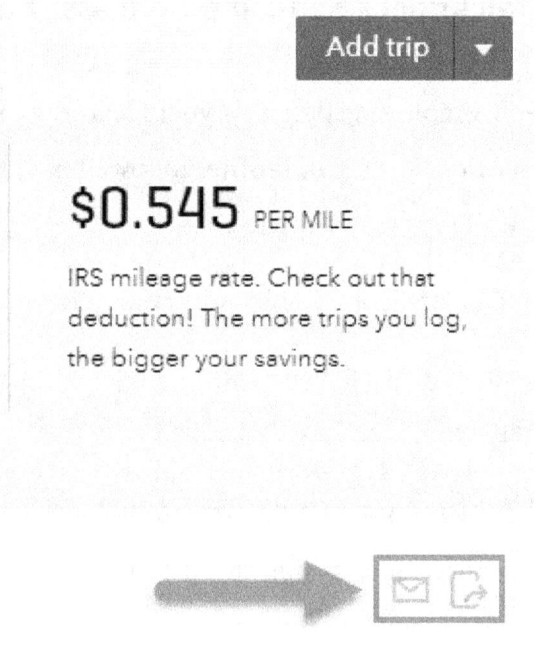

How would I share my reports with my bookkeeper?

You can email them your downloaded reports or welcome your bookkeeper to your QuickBooks on the off chance that they use QuickBooks for Accountants. Here's the ticket:

1. Sign in to QuickBooks Self-Employed.
2. Go to Settings.
3. Select the Accountant.
4. Enter your bookkeeper's email address.
5. Select Send Invite.

What is a duty deduction?

In case you're recording, you've independently employed taxes just because as the aftereffect of beginning another business, you're likely thinking about what precisely a tax deduction is.

A duty reasoning is a measure of cash; the Internal Revenue Service enables you to subtract from your Adjusted Gross Income (AGI) to lessen your taxable pay. At times, taking enough tax deductions can put you in a lower personal tax section, significantly diminishing the measure of duties you pay every year.

There are two essential kinds of findings accessible under the United States charge law: the standard deduction and ordered reasonings.

The vast majority will choose to take the standard expense finding course. This is a level sum the IRS gives you a chance to deduct from your duty charge, no questions asked. The measure of the standard derivation shifts dependent on your recording status.

For the 2018 assessment year, the duty code stipulates that single taxpayers and married taxpayers documenting independently can guarantee a $12,000 standard reasoning sum for the 2018 expense year. Those wedded recording mutually can guarantee a $24,000 standard conclusion, and citizens documenting as "head of a family unit" — that is, single people with wards — can guarantee a standard deduction of $18,000.

While accepting an expense finding of somewhere in the range of $12,000 to $24,000 may appear to be a ton, by deciding to separate deductions instead of taking the standard reasoning, specialists and other independently employed experts can frequently lessen their duty bill by a more prominent sum.

Itemized deductions incorporate a scope of costs that would somehow or another not be deductible. For independently employed people, these are costs that are viewed as "normal and essential" for leading business. These can run from promoting to utilities and everything in the middle. Keep in mind, however, that you can deduct the business-use part of the cost you're guaranteeing.

Why does it have to be so complicated?

While there may be a couple of motivations to begrudge the self-employed way of life, the expanded tax preparation burden isn't one of them. Self-employed experts face special difficulties when tax season comes around because they don't have charges retained from their checks like increasingly conventional full-time workers who document their duties with a straightforward W-2.

Not exclusively should a few freelancers record quarterly duty installments or hazard IRS punishments and expenses. However, they are additionally required to pay the segment of Medicare and Social Security commonly secured by a business, just as the bit that would be retained from a worker's check. The all-out Medicare and Social Security charges paid independently from anyone else utilized people are called independent work charges. Considering this more prominent budgetary weight, independently employed individuals need to exploit all conceivable duty conclusions to remain productive.

To offset the expense of working together individually terms, independently employed experts frequently depend intensely on tax deductions to reduce their tax rate. At the point when you separate your conclusions, the measure of those deductions is subtracted from your balanced gross pay, bringing about your taxable pay. At the point when you're ready to bring down your taxable salary, you additionally by and large reduction your duty bill. While utilizing independently employed duty findings positively isn't one-size-fits-all; there are some broad rules you can pursue to assist you with the beginning. While charge rules for consultants can be mind-boggling, independently employed experts can, for the most part, discount costs that fall into three classes:

1. Things you use exclusively in working your business.

2. Things you use throughout working together.
3. Things you use only for your business in the space where your business works.

Regular Deductions for the Independently Employed

This list is pertinent for some, independently employed experts. This may incorporate rideshare drivers, for example, Uber or Lift drivers, who guarantee huge mileage reasoning, or authors who may take the home office deduction. These business findings can also apply to creators, maids, picture takers, development laborers, specialists, or whatever other experts who work for themselves. Here are probably the most widely recognized reasoning.

Travel and hotel

If you travel to visit customers or go to public expos, you might have the option to deduct these costs. Business travel costs can incorporate transportation and convenience costs, and the IRS permits a half derivation for business supper costs. Note that you shouldn't endeavor to discount any costs related to sightseeing and recreation travel, which can trigger a review.

Home office

Numerous freelancers work out of their homes in the good 'old days, particularly when their organizations are first getting off the ground. Accordingly, the IRS permits independently employed people to deduct the segment of their home loan (counting property charges) or their lease that goes to a home office. To fit the bill for this discount, you should have a particular area in your home assigned for working, and you should avoid utilizing it for different purposes. While guaranteeing this reasoning, you can ascertain the finding's worth utilizing either the standard or simplified home office derivation alternative.

Utilities

While business owners with workplaces outside their homes can deduct 100% of their utilities, freelancers who work inside the home can, in any case, discount a bit of this expense as a major aspect of the home office cost. The level of your utility costs that are charge deductible is relative to the level of your home involved by your office.

Alongside gas and power, freelancers can deduct the expenses of warming, cooling, and telephone service. Know, notwithstanding, that you can't deduct the expense of utilities on the off chance that you guarantee the disentangled home office finding.

Professional development

As a freelancer, it's significant that you discover approaches to stand apart from your rivals in the business. To keep in front of the pack, numerous freelancers go to classes and instructive courses.

The expense of these costs can include, so the IRS enables consultants to deduct costs identified with proficient advancement on their taxes return. Moreover, independently employed people can discount their contribution to proficient associations and membership expenses.

Advertising and marketing

In our inexorably associated society, independently employed individuals need to take part in marketing and advertising if they would like to remain focused. The IRS grants freelancers to discount the expense of flyers, web notices, business cards, and print advertisements, among other promoting costs.

Website

With a larger part of shoppers utilizing the web to examine buys, making a mobile-friendly, responsive site is urgent for a freelancer's prosperity. Fortunately, independently employed people can deduct costs identified with their business sites, including area expenses, website composition, web building, and support.

Software

Nowadays, most consultants go through their days gazing at PC screens. From modern video altering projects to increasingly fundamental alternatives like Microsoft Office and Adobe Acrobat, programming can be costly. Hence, this is a valuable derivation for small business owners and freelancers.

Mileage and gas

Do you routinely drive to meet customers or providers? Provided that this is true, you should exploit the duty findings accessible for costs identified with vehicle mileage or typical vehicle mileage. You can pick between two kinds of vehicle-related derivations: the standard mileage choice or the genuine cost alternative.

The standard mileage alternative enables you to make reasoning dependent on what number of miles you've utilized for business purposes. The genuine cost choice enables you to make sense of the amount it costs you to keep up and work your vehicle explicitly for business use.

Incorporation

If your independent business is fruitful, you might be considering consolidating soon. The IRS allows new organizations to deduct uses related to incorporation, including state charges and lawful expenses during the business' first year of activity. Before you change your structure, notwithstanding, be certain you not just adjust it to the assessment and legal codes, yet additionally, your own field-tested strategy for development.

Self-employment health insurance deduction

Most full-time workers get their medical coverage through their manager. However, numerous independently employed experts must pay compensation for their medicinal services out of pocket, and those month to month premiums can mean a weighty wad of cash each month.

Fortunately, independently employed people who meet certain criteria might be qualified for an extraordinary tax deduction that enables them to deduct 100% of any health insurance premiums paid to an insurance agency, including dental costs, vision, and long-and transient consideration — for themselves, their life partners, and any family members.

If you meet the accompanying necessities, you can deduct up to the full cost of your medical coverage plan:

- Your business is guaranteeing a benefit. If your business asserts a misfortune for the assessment year, you can't guarantee this deduction.
- You were not qualified to select a business' health plan. This likewise incorporates your life partner's arrangement. If you were qualified to join up with one and decided not to, you can't guarantee this finding.
- You are possibly endeavoring to guarantee premiums paid for the months when you were not qualified for a business's health plan.

Note this isn't, carefully, a business finding. Rather, it is ordered by the IRS as an exceptional individual conclusion for the independently employed. Like this, it applies just to your government charges, state assessments, and nearby personal duties, and not to your independent work charges.

How Do Those Deductions Translate Into Paperwork?

A portion of the self-employment tax deductions above may not matter to your calling. However, you may be shocked by the number that does. At the point when you're prepared to record, you'll list most of your conclusions in Part II of your Schedule C (Form 1040). On the off chance that you have under $5,000 in claims, you might have the option to utilize Schedule C-EZ.

Learn the Basics About QuickBooks File Manager

QuickBooks File Manager is an independent application for QuickBooks Accountant and QuickBooks Enterprise Accountant. It stores organization records, together with usernames and passwords, in a safe domain. The application enables you to import customer's QuickBooks documents and effectively upgrade starting with one QuickBooks form then onto the next.

You can get to QuickBooks File Manager through a symbol from your work area or the Accountant menu in QuickBooks Accountant Editions.

Note:

- The Password Vault of the QuickBooks File Manager can be utilized to deal with the complex passwords that numerous records currently require.
- If a similar list of documents and their login/secret phrase is required on numerous PCs, the File Manager reinforcement can be utilized and reestablished on different PCs.

What would you be able to do in QuickBooks File Manager?

- Build a customer list that makes a virtual perspective on your hard drive, bunches customers' QuickBooks documents by type, and contains areas of customers' organization records.
- Save login data for your customers; QuickBooks records in the Password Vault gives you a chance to open a customer's document from the customer list and without looking at the login data upward.
- Upgrade different customers' QuickBooks records to the most recent variant of QuickBooks in a clump.
- Create Groups of customers that you characterize.

How can it work?

- It arranges customer envelopes and organizations in an easy to use an index that is based on the client's unique direction.
- It bunches all the organization records for every customer into their specific configuration (.QBW, .QBB, .QBA, and .QBM) for simplicity of association.
- It recollects the username and secret phrase for each document for a simple opening of the record when choosing to open the record from File Manager.

Three different ways to begin QuickBooks File Manager

- On QuickBooks Accountant menu, select QuickBooks File Manager.
- On your Desktop, click the QuickBooks File Manager symbol.
- From the Windows Start menu, go to Programs > QuickBooks > File Manager.

Note: Access the most recent QuickBooks File Manager introduced.

Two different ways to import QuickBooks records

- On the QuickBooks File Manager, go to Clients drop-down and pick Add Clients using, at that point, select Update Client List Wizard.
- Import From customer envelope names, if you have just sorted out the organization documents and envelopes into an arrangement exactly as you would prefer.
- Import from QuickBooks record names, on the off chance that you have not sorted out your documents and envelopes, and you need the File Manager to filter your PC and import the records. It will also name the records equivalent to how they are named on your PC or system.
- Drag and drop the records from Windows File Explorer into File Manager.

Open the organization record from File Manager

- You can double click on the document or go to Files drop-down; at that point, select Open in QuickBooks.

Note: Two records can also be opened immediately through the document chief (when utilizing the bookkeeper release.)

- You may also changeover/reestablish records. Go to Files > Restore to QBW, or Convert to QBA.

Manage and Merge customer folders

- You can see your assembled customers into favored gatherings dependent on your customers.
- QuickBooks File Manager naturally bunches the documents by year in the Groups dropdown.
- You can deal with your gatherings by going to Groups > Add/Edit groups or Delete Current gathering when a group is chosen.
- You may also look through customers by any predetermined term with the search option.
- You can merge customer envelopes by choosing the two folders, right-click at that point pick Merge chose clients.

Note: It groups every one of the records forms all folders that were consolidated, bringing about no lost documents.

- You may also deal with the customer organizers and records from the Files dropdown.
- When a customer is chosen from the customer list, data will populate in the "Documents" area to one side. After a record has been opened through the File Manager, document data will populate in the "Data" tab that is to one side of the "Documents tab."

Password Vault

- The Password vault saves your username and secret phrase for any organization record you have.
- You can deal with your saved passwords by going to Password Vault.

Note: This will demand confirmation.

- You may also deal with your Password Vault login data from Password Vault > Change Password Vault login. To keep it verified, Password Vault requires the client to make a client name and password before adding customer documents to it.

Batch Upgrade (Does not apply to the UK)

- Batch upgrade incredibly diminishes the hour of updating organization records by overhauling every single chosen document on the double.
- You can batch records by going to Batch Upgrade > Clients > Upgrade chose files. Note: You'll have the option to see every

single ineffective update inside this window by choosing List unsuccessful Upgrades.

File Manager backup

The file manager has an accessible reinforcement framework that spares your settings and catalogs, so if you experience information loss, and it tends to be reestablished to the latest backup similarly as you left it.

Resolve QuickBooks Desktop execution issues: Manage your information record

If you are having issues with the presentation of your QuickBooks Desktop, your organization document might be the root cause. You have alternatives you can use to determine such issues.

QuickBooks' performance diminishes as the size of the organization record increments. There are no genuine cutoff points on the size of your organization's information document. However, performance might be blocked if your system isn't fit for taking care of large information files.

Recommendations to Resolve Performance Issues

Reduce the size of the company file

If you have a huge record and execution is slower than what is required, you can decrease the size of your organization document. Know that these alternatives are difficult and require a great deal of time and work. You can:

Run the Condense Data Utility. See The Condense Data utility for guidelines.

Truncate your organization record. This ability isn't worked into QuickBooks, nor intuits offer truncation as a different help. You can evacuate exchanges up to a chose date and afterward set up opening adjustments as of that date. You can truncate by (1) Sending your organization document to a third-party seller OR (2) Obtaining third party information move, and opening adjusts applications. For us, truncating your record in a past schedule year should not influence DIY with DD payroll if you have Assisted Payroll, counsel Payroll Support before truncating your record.

Start another organization record.

The US: Starting another organization document won't influence Desktop Payroll DIY with Direct Deposit. If you have Assisted Payroll, counsel Payroll Support before beginning another record.

- If you choose to begin another organization document, you have two alternatives:
1. Use the Condense Company Data choice to erase all exchanges. This leaves you with a shell that has just your lists. (Concerns US as it were)
2. Create another record without any preparation. This sounds simple, yet is possibly a great deal of work and will require some investment.
   a. In the old record, go to File > New Company. Follow the wizard that shows up.
   b. In the old record, send out your lists. Open the documents and tidy them up by erasing idle or never again required lists entries. See Export or import IIF records for steps to trade your lists.
   c. Import the cleaned documents into the new record. See IIF Overview: import unit, test records, and headers.
   d. Set up the opening adjustments. Go to the QuickBooks App Store to discover utilities that will do this for you.

Set organization and personal preferences

Organization Preferences

1. Log in to your organization record as the Administrator.
2. If in multi-client mode, go to File > Switch to Single User Mode.
3. Once in single-client mode, go to the Edit, and afterward, pick Preferences.
4. From the left menu, select Bills.
5. Select the Company Preferences Tab.

- a. Clear the Warn about copy charge numbers from a similar vendor checkbox.
- b. Select yes in the Save Changes window.
6. From the left menu, pick Items and Inventory.
- a. Clear the Warn about copy to buy request numbers.
- b. Click yes in the Save Changes window.
7. From the left menu, pick Sales and Customers. Clear these checkboxes:
- Warn about copy receipt numbers.
- Warn about copy Sales Order numbers.
- Click yes in the Save Changes window.
8. From the left menu, pick Search.
- a. Clear the Update automatically checkbox.
- b. Click yes in the Save Changes window.
- c. When the entirety of the organization's preferences is set, click OK.

Individual Preferences

1. Go to the Edit menu and then pick Preferences.
2. Click the My Preferences Tab.
3. From the left menu, I have picked Desktop View.
- a. Select don't spare the desktop option.
- b. Clear the Show Home page when opening the organization record checkbox.
- c. Clear the Show Getting Started checkbox.
- d. Click yes in the Save Changes window.

1. From the left menu, picked General.
a. Select the Keep QuickBooks running for snappy new businesses checkbox.
b. Click yes in the Save Changes window.

Note: This choice is a tradeoff:

- If checked, QuickBooks begins quicker, yet may run more slowly.
- If unchecked, QuickBooks begins more slowly, however, it may run quicker.

2. From the left menu, picked Reminders.
   a. Clear the Show Reminders List when opening a Company File checkbox.
b. Click yes in the Save Changes window.
6. From the left menu, picked Reports and Graphs.
   a. In the Reports and Graphs area, pick Don't Refresh.

Note: Reports will refresh just when you decide to do as such. This preference can build your performance if you have a few reports open while you are entering exchanges.

b. Click to choose the Prompt me to change report choices before opening a report checkbox.

7. When the entirety of your preferences is set, click OK.

Automatic Updates

1. From the Help menu, pick Update QuickBooks.

2. Click the Options tab.

3. In the Automatic Updates segment, select no.

4. Click Close.

5. Click OK.

Optimize QuickBooks operations

1. Reduce your DB File Fragments. Excessive DB File Fragments can degrade the performance of your PC. See Database (DB) document sections for more data.

2. Resort your Master Name List (clients, sellers, workers, and different names), your Chart of Accounts, and your Item List. Do this to your lists week by week. Use steps from Qbwin.log: Verify Account Balance failed.

3. Verify your organization record week after week. See Resolve information damage on your organization record.

4. Transaction log records (TLG) monitor changes to the document since the last backup. Enormous TLG documents can cause performance issues. In any case, don't erase the TLG record. Rather, make a manual backup with a full check to reset the TLG.

5. Since QuickBooks Desktop re-lists the information while reestablishing a convenient organization document, make and reestablish a compact organization record. See Create or reestablish a QuickBooks convenient organization record for details.

6. Do not enter zero lines on exchanges. A zero line (with a zero cost or amount) adds another objective to your information document and builds the size of your information record. Zero lines moderate QuickBooks' exhibition and, if you run money premise reports with stock, your COGS could be inaccurate.

7. Run accrual reports rather than money: Many exchanges, for example, more than 50,000, will, in general, debase the Sybase Sequel server. Money basis reports take more time to run because QuickBooks must check transactions connects to figure out what is paid and unpaid.

8. If QuickBooks runs gradually while doing payroll, have different clients log off and perform payroll tasks in single-client mode.

9. Close QuickBooks windows that you are not at present utilizing.

10. Clear the lines of forms to be printed or messaged.

11. If you are the main client in the information record, change to single-client mode.

12. Reboot your workstations day by day.

13. Log out of the information record if you are not effectively utilizing it and don't remain signed into the organization document medium-term

14. Perform long undertakings in off-top hours (email or print groups of invoices or statements) in the off-hours (before typical hours, noon or overnight), so they don't take assets from different clients.

15. Optimize reports. Running reports is a serious QuickBooks activity as it draws together a great deal of information. Advancing detailing and printing reports can spare a significant measure of time and assets. The Sales Tax Liability Report and the General Ledger report will, in general, belong reports. Here are a few hints:

- Run long reports in the off-hours, during lunch, medium-term, throughout the end of the week.
- Customize and remember long reports.
- Copy your organization document to an unused workstation, set the driver to print directly to the printer, and print your report.

16. Turn off the built-in search ordering in QuickBooks Desktop (Edit > Preferences > Search > Company Preferences > (Uncheck) Update Automatically) and rename the <Filename>.qbw.SearchIndex folder.

IMPORTANT:

- <Filename>.qbw.SearchIndex organizer is automatically made when QuickBooks Desktop search inclination is set to program. The contents of this organizer are used by the program to run a brisk filed search when you press F3 in an organized document.
- You can, at present, search in your organization record in the wake of turning the inherent pursuit ordering off. However, it will take longer. If killing this component didn't improve the performance of the program, it is highly recommended to walk out on.

- You can discover the .qbw.SearchIndex organizer in a similar area as your organization file.

Example:

C:\Users\Public\PublicDocuments\Intuit\QuickBooks\CompanyFIles\CompanyFileName.qbw.SearchIndex

Maintain lists

Before you start, play out the following:

1. Create a backup of your information document.

2. be aware that once two sections are consolidated, the union cannot be fixed.

3. Create a document duplicate of your record. If you blend any rundown passages, open the file duplicate to see the historical backdrop of the merged sections.

List characteristics that can hinder performance

- Your records are moving toward as far as possible. Study the most extreme number of list sections (list cutoff points and custom fields).
- Your records have countless inert sections that you never again use.
- Your client list has numerous occupations underneath clients.
- Your account list has many sub-accounts.
- Your thing list has many sub-items.

- The Customer, Vendor, and Employee focuses have uniquely arranged name records.

Custom Sorted Lists

1. Open the Center (Customer Center, Vendor Center, and so forth.) that has performance issues.

2. To the left of the Name section, guarantee there is no diamond column.

3. If there is a diamond column, click the diamond to evacuate it. You shouldn't be in a single-client mode to expel the diamond.

4. Close the Center and revive it.

Modify Lists

Graph of Accounts: If you are utilizing sub-records to follow the source of payor utilization of costs, consolidate sub-accounts or into the parent records and set up Classes to do the following.

Thing List: Merge old as well as idle things that are never again sold. Combined things lose their character; be certain you have an archive copy with the historical backdrop of everything.

Client List: If you're Customer: Job list has a few old employments underneath Customers, combine them. If you have old, inert Customers to whom you never again sell, merge them. The merged clients and positions lose their personality; be certain you have a document copy with their individual history.

Employee List: If you have old, inert Employees whom you never again utilize, combine them. The merged employees lose their personality; be certain you have a file copy with their individual history and be certain that you have the entirety of their tax documents modern, printed, and submitted to the suitable tax agencies.

Move your Company Files to Another Computer

Figure out how to move your organization documents to another organizer on your PC, on and off your system, or to another PC.

Need to move your organization documents around? You may need to move them in case you're investigating or moving your accounting information to another PC.

The easiest route is to make and restore a backup organization record since it spares your information and supporting documents. You can also basically reorder your whole QuickBooks organizer to another area.

If you use QuickBooks Desktop as a single client (which means you don't have your organization documents on a system), there's a simple method to move everything. Follow these means to utilize the Migrator Tool.

Move your organization record to another PC

Note: Moving your organization document to another PC won't influence your item license.

1. Before you start, ensure you introduce QuickBooks Desktop on the new PC.

2. Follow the means to make a backup organization document on your unique PC.

3. When you spare the backup document, give it an extraordinary name, so it's anything but difficult to distinguish. This also prevents accidental overwrites.

4. Save the backup record someplace you can undoubtedly think that it, similar to your Windows work area.

5. Move the backup organization record to your new PC. You can either put the reinforcement on a flash drive or an external device. Or then again you can share it if your new PC is on a similar system.

6. Follow the means to reestablish the backup on your new PC. Keep in mind, and it ought to have a special record name.

7. If you use payroll, download the most recent expense table after you move your record.

Move your organization document to another area on a similar PC

If you need to move your organization record to another organizer or area:

1. Follow the means to make a backup organization document.

2. When you save the backup, give it a one of a kind name, so it's anything but difficult to distinguish. This additionally prevents accidental overwrites.

3. Save the backup someplace you can without much of a stretch think that it, similar to your Windows desktop. Note: If your

organization record is facilitated on a system, save the backup on your PC's neighborhood hard drive. Try not to save it on your system.

4. Follow the means to restore the backup to the new envelope or area. Keep in mind, and it ought to have a unique filename. After you restore the backup, use it as your new principal organization document. We additionally suggest renaming your unique organization record.

Include "old" to the filename, so you know not to utilize it any longer.

Move custom formats and structures that aren't a piece of the backup

Alternative: Move your whole QuickBooks information folder

As another option, if you would prefer not to make a backup organization record, you can move your whole QuickBooks folder.

1. Open QuickBooks and the organization record you need to move.

2. Press F2 (or Ctrl+1) to open the Product Information window.

3. Look in the File Information area. This reveals to you where your organization record is saved money on your hard drive.

4. Open the Windows Start menu and afterward open File Explorer.

5. Find the organizer that has your organization record.

6. Right-click the organizer and select Copy.

7. Open the external device you'll use to move the documents or open the new area on your hard drive. At that point, select Paste.

You presently have a copy of your whole organizer. You can move it to your new PC or another area on your hard drive. At that point open QuickBooks and select

Open or Restore a current organization. Follow your PC for the organizer; you just replicated and opened the copied organization document.

Solution 4: Restore using Intuit Data Protect

Note: Depending on your Intuit Data Protect (IDP) plan (single document or whole PC), some non-QuickBooks records may not be sponsored up. Visit Intuit App Center for more data about your IDP memberships.

1. Follow the means to make a backup of your organization document on your unique PC.

2. Sign in to IDP on your new PC.

3. Follow the means to restore the backup document utilizing IDP.

The accompanying documents are moved and restored:

Documents inside QuickBooks information folder:

- Logos and pictures documents
- Transaction log (.tlg) documents
- Network information (.nd) documents

- Cash Flow Projector (.cfp) documents
- Loan Manager (.lmr) documents
- Business Planner (.bpw) documents (QuickBooks Desktop Premier and Enterprise as it were)

Records (and additional items) from different areas:

- QuickBooks letters and formats
- Spell checker
- Fixed Asset Manager
- Printer setting (These records can be reproduced by QuickBooks)
- QuickBooks Statement Writer (Premier Accountant and Enterprise as it were)

How to Set Up a New Sales Tax Code

Immediately set up another business charge code by following a couple of basic advances.

1. From the left menu, select Taxes.

2. Select Sales Tax. (Tip: If you use finance in QuickBooks Online, you may need to choose Sales Tax instead of Payroll Tax.)

3. Select Manage deals charge.

4. Select Add charge.

5. Under what sort of tax would you like to include? Select Add alongside one of the below alternatives and pursue the prompts to finish setting up.

For Provincial:

- This choice will consequently set up any new organizations fundamental, (for example, new PST offices) and the most well-known codes for that region/domain.
- It will provoke you to pick an area or domain starting from the drop. (Tip: Only regions that you haven't yet set up will be recorded.)

For Group rate:

- This choice will give you a chance to consolidate any current duty codes into a "combo rate."
- For extra data on bunch deals, charge rates look at how would I include a group deals charge rate?
- For more data on one of the most widely recognized gathering rates, look at How to set up a business charge rate for Meals and Entertainment.

For Custom:

- This choice is once in a while utilized, since any code recorded along these lines will unequivocally not answer to any Federal or Provincial Tax Agencies (i.e., Canada Revenue Agency, Receiver General, etc.), and won't help with documenting/answering to these sorts of offices.
- You can include an expense in this classification explicit to your industry, for example, tobacco, inn, or gas charge. It could also be utilized to follow deals with U.S. clients. Another utilization could be to set up a legitimate "out-of-scope" charge code to demonstrate that the deal/cost doesn't fall under any tax if the organization doesn't have one in any way, shape, or form.
- The custom charge must be in a rate position, not a specific dollar amount.

How to add a custom sales tax rate for an existing sales tax agency

This alternative will enable you to physically set up an expense for one of the current offices (i.e., Receiver General, Canada Revenue Agency, etc.). Consider the following:

- This can be utilized for charge rate changes and other extraordinary duty rates.
- It's smarter to include an extra expense code than to change the current one (along these lines, all business charge rates for that office would appear on a similar return).

1. From the left menu, select Taxes.

2. Select Sales Tax at the top. (Tip: If you use finance in QuickBooks Online, you may need to choose Sales Tax rather than Payroll Tax.)

3. Select Manage deals charge.

4. Locate the business charge office you wish to include the new rate for, and select Add custom rate.

That is it. You presently realize how to set up another business charge code.

Alter Sales Tax Rate in QuickBooks Online

Did you get a notification that your business charge rate is evolving? Here are how to transform it into QuickBooks Online:

To edit Sales Tax Rates:

1. Go to Taxes from the menu, at that point pick Sales Tax.

2. Under Related Tasks, select Add/edit tax rates and agencies.

3. In the Sales Tax Rates and Agencies table, pick the rate you need to change and choose Edit.

4. In the Edit Sales Tax Component window, change the rate. You can likewise change the part name if you like.

5. Choose Save. When done, it comes back to the business Tax rates and Agencies table and features the rate you changed.

What happens when you edit a sales tax rate?

- The new rate is accessible for new exchanges as it were
- If you make another exchange, however, use dates previously, the exchange utilizes the new rate
- After you alter a rate, the previous rate can never again be utilized
- Existing transactions that utilized the previous rate stay unaltered except if you alter the transaction and explicitly select an alternate deal charge rate
- For repeating layouts that utilization the changed segment, new transactions made with the format utilize the new rate. Existing transactions made with the format, and the previous rate stays unchanged

- Reports show the information for the two rates (previously, then after the fact) if there are exchanges for both the rates in a specific period

Look at QuickBooks Sales Tax

If you have ever purchased or sold anything or attempted to help your customers with anything identified with their sales transactions, you have more than likely experienced deals charge. For simple buys, deals charge is the keep going detail on a receipt that appears to make all that you purchase more costly. Taking a look at it on a receipt, deals charge appears to be basic, yet it can become complicated immediately when you are the business owner or a bookkeeper helping a business owner. There are about 11,000 sales tax and more than 60,000 deals charge rules controlling the assortment of offers charge in the United States and barely any assets for independent companies or accountants to go to guarantee appropriate computation and consistency.

All in all, the business charge is determined to utilize five snippets of data identified with the deal:

1. **Location:** One of the most significant factors in figuring a business charge rate is the area of a deal. For deals that happen over the counter, the location of the business is utilized to decide the rate. If a business is delivering or sending an item to an area other than their place of business, be that as it may, the expense can be founded either on the ship from address or the ship-to address contingent upon the sourcing rules of the state(s) engaged with the deal.

2.   **Nexus:** Knowing where there is a commitment to gather and remit tax is additionally applicable because an organization may not generally need to gather deals charge in each state where they have deals. For deals into states where a business doesn't have nexus, for instance, there is no commitment to gather deals charge on the exchange. In these states, the client is rather answerable for reporting these deals on their annual assessment form as use charge. To decide if your organization has nexus in some random state, allude to the guidelines set out by that state's Tax Agency or counsel with a duty consultant or lawyer.

3.   **Product:** The things you decide to sell can change the business charge rate you need to charge on an exchange. Products and services are not taxed consistently over the US. For instance, a few states absolve or diminish rate certain need things, for example, nourishment, clothing, or therapeutic things from deals charge. In different states, services might be absolved, or the states may have a rundown of things where charges may apply. Eight instances of how the sale tax of a simple lemon can change contingent upon what the last item being sold are in the Sales Tax of a Lemon.

4.   **Customer:** Who you are offering to can also change the assessment rate for a given exchange. Things can go from completely taxable to completely exclude if the client creates a legitimate exemption certificate. Each state offers a one of a kind arrangements of substance and use-based exclusions that are accessible to buyers. Continuously make sure to gather that exemption certificate.

5. **Date:** The date of a business exchange can influence the rate that is applied. Deals charge rates are consistently changing, particularly at the local level. Not exclusively do states, urban communities, areas, and regions change deals charge rates periodically. However, numerous states additionally have deals charge occasions on different occasions consistently.

How QuickBooks Sales Tax Works

QuickBooks Sales Tax makes figuring, gathering, following, and transmitting deals charge increasingly helpful. The element right now supports clients on collection accounting.

Here are how it works:

Set up deals charge: Customers can set up deals charge by visiting the duties tab in QuickBooks. They should confirm their street number and record which charge offices they are registered with.

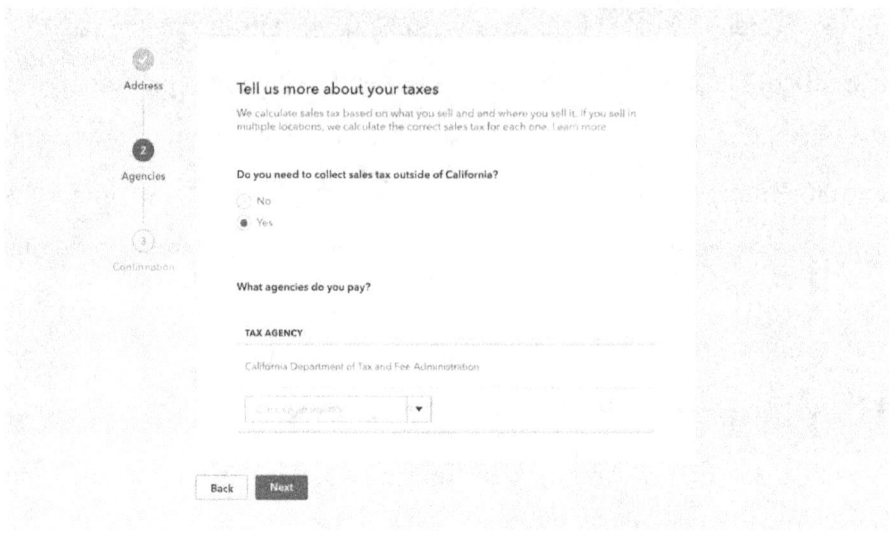

Create an invoice: Customers can incorporate deals charge on a receipt by entering client data, classifying their items/services, and checking them as assessable. Except if shipping data is given, QuickBooks Sales Tax will utilize the organization address for a default rate.

See the sales tax breakdown: Once a client has remembered an assessable item for a receipt, they will have the option to perceive how the rate figuring and breakdown by tapping on the sales tax drawer. Clients are additionally ready to make changes from the sales tax drawer.

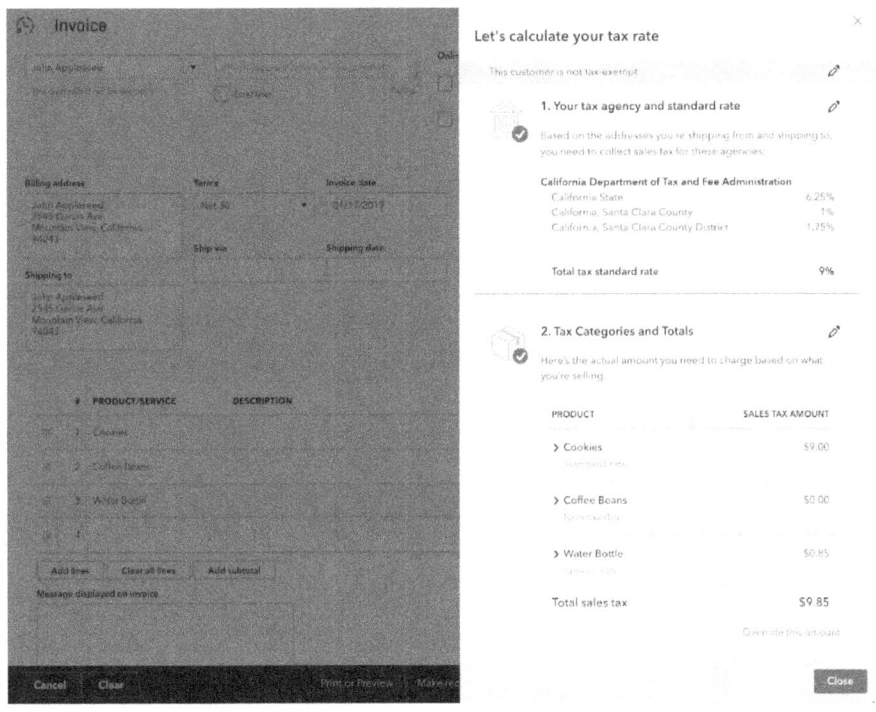

Documenting: Customers who track deals charge through QuickBooks are given a choice to record and pay through QuickBooks electronically. Note that not all states are right now upheld for e-filing.

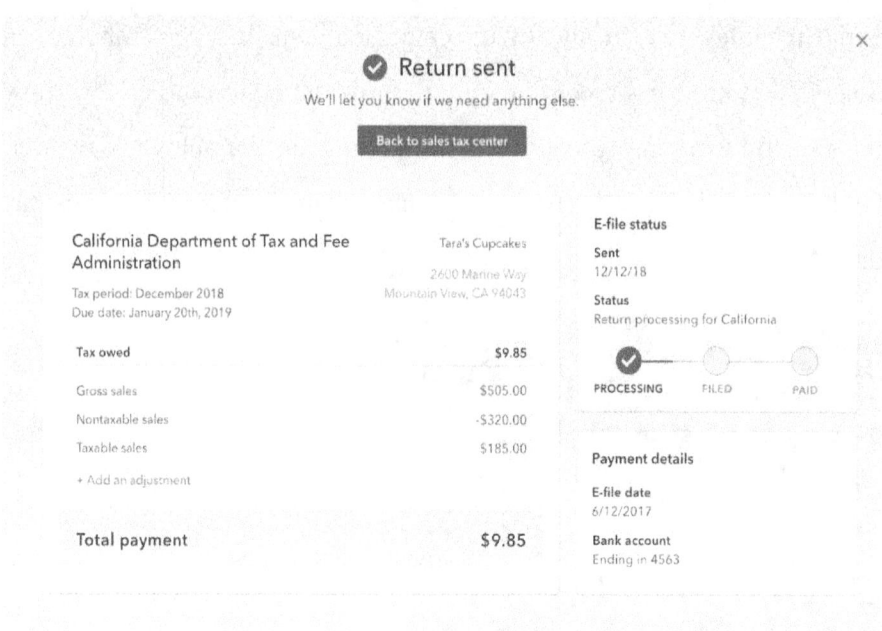

QuickBooks Sales Tax assists clients with saving time and deal with their business charge commitments by giving the most exact principles, rates, and recording services. This usefulness is particularly useful for clients utilizing invoices or sales receipts. There is no more need to follow the paces of the 11,000 taxing purviews or 60,000 duty rules since deals charge rates and rules are consequently refreshed as changes become effective. For instance, numerous states executed deals charge decide and rate changes that were effective on Jan. 1, 2019. These progressions were conveyed to QuickBooks Sales Tax clients, yet there was nothing more for these clients to do than read the correspondence.

Clients can trust QuickBooks Sales Tax to assist them with remaining present and agreeable with regards to deals charge. You can discover increasingly point by point data on the most proficient method to set up QuickBooks Sales Tax here.

*Supported States		
Arkansas	Michigan	Rhode Island
California	Minnesota	South Carolina
Connecticut	Nebraska	South Dakota
DC	Nevada	Tennessee
Florida	New Jersey	Texas
Georgia	New Mexico	Utah
Indiana	North Carolina	Vermont
Iowa	North Dakota	Virginia
Kentucky	Ohio	West Virginia
Maine	Oklahoma	Wisconsin
Massachusetts	Pennsylvania	Wyoming

Need to Learn QuickBooks for Free?

In the event that you request that a random individual name the principal accounting software that rings a bell, QuickBooks will probably be their answer.

Intuit's QuickBooks surprised the business world, soaring to fame (particularly in private company circles) and landing decisively on the platform saved for all product unicorns.

Indeed, even today, with such a large number of programming options accessible, QuickBooks is still observed as being similarly as brilliant, shiny, and rainbow-colored as it was numerous years prior. Furthermore, that has helped this amazing unicorn (sporting the exemplary green-related to the organization) stay number one.

Over 4.3 million clients depend on QuickBooks. Also, that makes having a strong comprehension of how the product functions a quintessential skill for private company owners and numerous accountants.

In any case, in case you're maintaining a business, you probably won't have the assets accessible to commit to paid preparation. Fortunately, there are approaches to figure out how to cause this unicorn to sing for you without big financial investment on your part.

Here are 11 resources to get you started:

1. QuickBooks Tutorials

At the point when you're searching for data on a program, once in a while, it's ideal to go to the unicorn that started everything. Intuit, the creator of QuickBooks, offers simple to pursue video instructional exercises for independent companies and accountants that utilization the product. The data is highly open and intended to assist you in achieving a wide assortment of tasks easily.

2. QuickBooks Learning Center

Another incredible source of data gave by Intuit is through the QuickBooks Learning Center. This element is remembered for the product through the assistance menu.

You can get to speedy learning modules, download PDF directs, and associate with different clients for direction all through this learning entrance.

3. QuickBooks-Training.net

While this website principally centers on paid preparing alternatives, they additionally give access to free online courses.

QuickBooks clients might be particularly inspired by the QB Power Hour, and an online course arrangement concentrated on giving watchers the abilities they have to become QuickBooks control clients.

Extra online classes center on well-known themes like charges and different tips that can assist you with benefiting from the program.

4. QuickBooks Training

QuickBooks Training is a second site that focuses on paid alternatives, yet additionally gives access to free how-to-style instructional exercises and articles.

A large portion of the free substance is equipped towards beginners, with recordings being just a couple minutes long, so it very well may be an extraordinary spot to begin if you have to take a few to get back some grip on the fundamentals.

5. Fit Small Business

Isolated into seven exercises, Fit Small Business gives a wide scope of data in digestible chunks.

Altogether, there are 39 video instructional exercises available covering such themes as "how to physically enter business Mastercard transactions," "how to deal with skipped checks from clients," and "how to run a records payable maturing report."

In total, these contributions are more intensive than some others, so it's a solid choice for the individuals who need to burrow somewhat deeper than the surface.

6. GCF Learn Free

GFCLearnFree.org is known for its free learning instructional exercises. It gives access to some QuickBooks assets intended to assist you with beginning with the work area or online versions of the product.

The data gave essential and even incorporates guidance for obtaining the program.

In case you're beginning from the earliest starting point, it could be an extraordinary stop. Be that as it may, any individual who has just done some underlying set up might be ideally serviced by different sources.

7. QuickBooks Explained

Another source of video instructional exercises, QuickBooks Explained, adopts an alternate strategy in regard to the structure of the data. A portion of the sections are longer, so they are more far-reaching than the contributions at certain different locales.

There are additionally shorter recordings for taking care of explicit tasks, giving you an option in contrast to the more drawn out structure fragments.

QuickBooks Explained also has a newsletter that may remember data about new improvements for the product so that it could merit investigating also.

8. Udemy

Udemy is an enormous scale learning stage, consolidating access to free and paid classes. The QuickBooks contributions that you can access at no expense shift in themes, with some being general and others being task explicit.

In contrast to some different stages, you can peruse client surveys (when accessible) to assist you with choosing if a course is directly for you, and you can also perceive what number of individuals are taking the class now.

New classes might be made whenever, so don't be hesitant to inquire consistently to see the most recent course contributions that may become available.

9. Dummies

A great many people know about the Dummies brand because of the accommodating instructional and data book arrangement that put the organization on the map. In any case, numerous individuals don't understand you can get to data and articles online for nothing.

While the substance isn't as comprehensive as you would discover in the most current variants of the books, there is a great deal of supportive data in there, some of which is in instructional exercise structure.

A quick search yielded more than 1,000 titles related to QuickBooks, so you may have the option to discover insights regarding further developed methods here.

10. Better Bottom Line

Better Bottom Line has various free PDF guides that emphasis more on data and less on direct guidance.

However, there are helpful aides for realizing what's going on in the most recent version of QuickBooks just as FAQs about upgrades.

11. LinkedIn Learning

While this site isn't, in fact, free, you can get a 30-day free trial that can assist you with getting a great deal of QuickBooks (and other) preparing at no expense.

Ways QuickBooks Can Help Run Your Small Business

QuickBooks is magnificent accounting programming for maintaining a small business. I like to tell customers that QuickBooks is incredible for a small business that doesn't get bookkeeping. The explanation I state this is a considerable lot of the accounting sections are done in the background in QuickBooks just via doing the everyday exercises of your business. Moreover, I also observe a ton of entrepreneurs not utilize QuickBooks to its maximum capacity. Here are 20 different ways QuickBooks can help maintain your independent company.

1. **Control Cash Flow** - QuickBooks can be an extraordinary device to assist you in dealing with your income. Rather than utilizing your online bank balance, you should keep your QuickBooks document normally refreshed and see how to utilize it to deal with your income. By entering your financial transactions regularly and doing day by day reconciliations in QuickBooks, you will get an incredible handle on your income. The key is arranging your QuickBooks bank accounts by cleared status.

2. **Receipt Customers** - I constantly prefer to prepare customers to make and send their invoices in QuickBooks. At the point when you have a client that needs to give you cash for items or administrations, that last thing you need to do is look

out for sending them a receipt, and figuring out how to appropriately receipt clients will diminish your records receivable and increment your income.

3. **Manage Bills and Accounts Payable** - Keeping your sellers and providers glad is significant too. You would prefer not to fall behind on your extraordinary bills with sellers. Utilizing the enter bills and take care of tabs works in QuickBooks is simple. Entering the bills to your sellers with the right terms and due dates will assist you with remaining over keeping your merchants paid and cheerful. Covering your tabs legitimately through QuickBooks using online bill pay or printing checks will decrease superfluous information passage and increment efficiency.

4. **Manage Employee Time** - You can enter a representative time from the worker's segment of the home screen. You can enter a solitary time occasion or utilize a week by week timesheet. The following time in QuickBooks can help measure worker efficiency and can demonstrate to be important for work costing purposes.

5. **Customized Chart of Accounts** - Your QuickBooks outline of records is about your needs and should be modified to those particular needs. I frequently observe customers make their outline of records so complicated that the reports become useless. Ensure your graph of records addresses you and gives you important data that you can utilize. Try not to stress a lot

overfitting your diagram of records to your expenses; it ought to be increasingly outfitted towards helping you maintain your business.

6. **Memorized Transactions** - You should utilize QuickBooks retained exchanges to consequently enter exchanges that happen on a standard and unsurprising premise. This can incorporate invoices, charges, diary passages, and installments. The thought is to help productivity and have certain things be entered naturally into QuickBooks. One case of a decent utilization of a retained exchange is a bill that you have set up to be consequently deducted from your financial records like your home loan installment. By remembering a check, you can have the installment naturally post to your financial records a specific number of days ahead of time.

7. **Always Reconciled** - The most significant thing you can accomplish for your private venture accounting framework is to try to reconcile QuickBooks on a predictable basis. You ought to accommodate the entirety of your material records, not simply your ledgers. Make a point to reconcile bank accounts, charge cards, advances, credit extensions, and financial liabilities.

8. **Printing Checks** - Printing checks from QuickBooks is an incredible method to keep income refreshed and increment your effectiveness. Since the check won't clear your bank until the payee stores it, you need to make a point to remember it for your

income investigation. Printing checks from QuickBooks will dispose of unnecessary information section.

9. **Web-based Banking** - You should set up your QuickBooks represents web-based banking download. Many major monetary organizations offer information downloads into QuickBooks. This will diminish a great deal of unnecessary data entry.

10. **Keep Questions Organized** - If you run over exchanges that you don't know how to deal with, don't give them a chance to prevent you from accommodating and finishing off your financials. Utilize the QuickBooks ask my accountant code on your graph of records. This will enable you to enter the transaction and accommodate all while keeping your questions sorted out in one spot.

11. **Journal Entries** - Journal passages are once in a while important to fix issues or make year-end sections per your CPA to coordinate your government form. Although dairy sections are getting more into the "bookkeeping" end of things, you should, at present, be familiar with them.

12. **Acknowledge Online Payments** - You can turn on the Intuit installment organize services, which enables clients to pay your invoices effectively on the web. The best part is it costs you $0.50 per exchange with no level of the receipt being charged as an expense. So you could send a $50,000 receipt and pay $0.50 to get that cash sent legitimately to your financial records.

Difficult to beat that value given the typical shipper preparing charges.

13. **Email Invoices and Statements** - You should set up all invoices and statements to be messaged directly from QuickBooks. This will help lessen the measure of time it takes for your clients to pay you, which will expand income. You can turn on the online installments as examined in #12 above to assist you with getting paid even faster.

14. **Payroll Management** - You can process your payroll legitimately in QuickBooks or utilize a re-appropriated payroll service. We typically prescribe redistributing your payroll to diminish your risk. At the point when you utilize a redistributed payroll, it is critical to record your outsourced payroll accurately in QuickBooks. Numerous finance organizations significantly offer records that can bring your outsourced payroll information into QuickBooks.

15. **QuickBooks Class Tracking** - QuickBooks class following is one of the more dominant elements of the product that regularly isn't used. QuickBooks classes are an approach to follow your information in a manner that is important to your business. Instances of QuickBooks classes are areas or divisions. I use QuickBooks classes to follow sources of salary with the goal that I know the source of each penny that our business has ever constructed.

16. **Financial Reporting -** One serious mix-up I see is private companies not exploiting the revealing that is accessible in QuickBooks. Independent company financial revealing is an essential bit of the accounting procedure. Without running and breaking down money related reports, your accounting framework isn't performing to its full capacity.

17. **Owner Memorized Reports -** I build up an exceptionally set of reports for myself to maintain our business. We additionally work with our customers to build up a lot of reports that the owner finds especially helpful to maintain their business. While numerous reports are accessible in QuickBooks, it is decent to sort out them across the board spot for simple access. Under Reports/Memorized Reports, you can discover your remembered report list. You ought to make another list called 'owner reports' and retain significant reports to that list to make them effectively open.

18. **Custom Importing -** If your monetary organization doesn't offer import capacities into QuickBooks regardless, and you have a few options. You can utilize a CSV converter to QuickBooks to make your information importable into QuickBooks. Furthermore, you can make Intuit Importable Files, also called IIF documents, which import into QuickBooks. You may need to look for an engineer or developer that can make IIF records.

19. **Web Apps** - There are a ton of applications that work with QuickBooks that may support your business. It merits browsing the applications to perceive how they can support your business. Make certain to get an application that is approved and supported by Intuit. One QuickBooks application that we as of late began utilizing is Time Tracker by eBillity. This application enables our workers to follow and enter their time from their PC, cell phone, or tablet. The administrator would then be able to approve the time, which would then be able to be set up to match up with your QuickBooks record.

20. **QuickBooks as a Tool** - Lastly, I need to discuss utilizing QuickBooks as a device to maintain your private company. Numerous small business owners take a look at accounting as a problem or as a way of recording their duties. I think some small business owners essentially don't care for accounting, others are threatened by it, and some don't see the incentive in it. If your accounting framework and QuickBooks record are set up appropriately and custom-fitted to your particular needs, they can assist you with maintaining your business. Your QuickBooks document ought to be a device that you can use to help you in settling on key business choices.

QuickBooks Tips to Simplify Your Life

QuickBooks is one of the most far-reaching accounting software packages available, and a large number of occupied entrepreneurs use it consistently. The product is famous for usability, a simple UX, security features, and rich bookkeeping features from the banking mix to worker the board. Nonetheless, getting up to speed on QuickBooks can be testing in case you're simply beginning utilizing it to sort out your funds. Regardless of whether you're a master at QuickBooks, you might be missing basic hints and deceives that can spare you hours every month adjusting the books and taking care of routine issues. How about we investigate 25 QuickBooks tips that can transform you and have your funds streamlined in a matter of moments.

Use ProAdvisor

Here's a tip for business owners simply beginning with QuickBooks: use ProAdvisor. ProAdvisor is a piece of the QuickBooks Intuit Package and associates you with a local accountant (contingent upon where you live) who can help get you fully operational on the product. They can also advise you on issues like duty necessities, balancing costs, and business structure.

Invest in Understanding the Basics

Like all software, QuickBooks expects to absorb information. In any case, if you utilize the Getting Started Tutorials that it offers, you'll be progressively alright with how this accounting software functions, for example, the board of bills, contributing expenses, and the sky is the limit from there. The instructional exercises are well-developed and exceptionally practical, so contribute two or three hours after you get set up familiarising yourself with the basic features.

Choose a Highly Secure Password

With regards to securing your money related information, the key has a strong password. This will save you a lot of cerebral pains later. Frequently, your QuickBooks coordinates with web-based banking; a hacked framework can dangerously open your financial vault. To change your password, visit the Your Account tab and go to Change Password.

Enter Correct Company Information

What your firm resembles, it's business structure, detailing structures, schedules for announcing just as its Tax ID number, is basic. Keep away from issues down the line by guaranteeing that every one of your information is entered accurately into the framework using the "Organization Tab." Inputting the right data and double-checking what's in the framework will assist you with getting the best proposals and results from the product.

Input Accurate Customer Details

Get familiar with the essentials of setting up a client in the framework. You should make ahead for the Customers Tab at the top focal point of your screen and enter all the client details. Info every client as another client and tweak their installment techniques, regardless of whether its money, check, or Visa. Setting up your center clients in a single sitting and being taught about including new clients as required makes it simpler to deal with assignments, for example, invoicing and reconciliation.

Inputting Employee Details

If you are utilizing this product to pay your employees, the product can assist you with overseeing payroll deductions, advantages, and tax payments. To exploit the component, visit the Employees Tab, which will lead you to the Employees Center. From that point, every worker can be immediately set up, and it's conceivable to see announcing.

Reconciling on QuickBooks

One of the necessary tips with QuickBooks that can change your life is steady reconciliation. At the point when you accommodate your records consistently, you generally have an elevated level of the image of what's going on in your business. It's basic: When you get an announcement or an installment settlement, guarantee it accommodates with your QuickBooks. This envelops all announcements, including those for charge cards, credits, and ledgers.

Backing up QuickBooks

Secure your information by backing up your QuickBooks. Set up a programmed timetable. Support up your QuickBooks is as basic as maintaining your business. You can't have your whole QuickBooks on one framework without support it up provided that it crashes, your data is lost. Use QuickBooks Online, and your information is automatically supported upon the Cloud. Something else, coordinate QuickBooks with your backup answer for additional security.

Print Checks Directly from QuickBooks

Printing checks can be costly and time-consuming. In case you're hoping to make your month to month reconciliations simpler, you should begin printing your very own minds QuickBooks. Go to the Banking Tab, and your first choice will be Write Checks. You would then be able to print. No all the more outsourcing or paying check expenses to your bank.

Paying Bills via QuickBooks

It's possible to streamline your business charge pay online through QuickBooks. This should be possible through the Online Bill Payment alternative. Not exclusively will you dispose of pointless advances, your life will be simpler with regards to accommodating your Accounts Payable.

Customize Your QuickBooks' Layout

The more up to date forms of QuickBooks have an alternate UI that is more adjustable than past versions. In any case, in case you're open to utilizing a more seasoned form and need to reproduce that format, or you essentially need to make a modification, you should go to Edit>Preferences>Desktop View.

Customize Your Icon Bar

Here's the beneficial thing about QuickBooks: You can alter what shows up on your Icon Bar. This makes it simpler to explore since you have the connections you require most. Head to View>Customize Icon Bar and keep what you utilize most regularly.

Use Memorized Transactions

Probably the ideal approach to make life less complex is to utilize QuickBooks to continue making ordinary transactions automatically. To empower that component, click on Lists>Memorized Transaction List>Memorized Transaction>New Group and set up the exchanges you need to be retained. You would then be able to utilize these to take care of tabs or send off the month to month invoices that pursue a similar example.

Utilize Online Banking

With QuickBooks, web-based banking turns into a reality, which streamlines coordinating your financial life. At the point when you utilize the QuickBooks Online Banking symbol on your Icon Bar, you'll be taken through an instructional exercise for web-based banking and can begin utilizing it immediately. Nonetheless, it's imperative to think about security; are there numerous clients that entrance the product who you don't need getting to your record?

Setting Up 1099 Vendors

Do you use temporary workers or independent assistance for your business? Provided that this is true, QuickBooks offers a component for setting up 1099 Vendors. This implies you'll have the option to sort your installments in addition to deals expenses to the self-employed entities of your business. It takes out the pressure-related to creating 1099s at year-end.

Turning Off Spellcheck

Spellcheck can be a bizarre element in QuickBooks, particularly when you're managing organization names. In case you're getting aggravated with Spellcheck, there's a method to turn it off. You should go to Edit>Preferences>Speller and uncheck the case for Always Check Spelling.

Limiting User Access

In the event that everybody is utilizing your QuickBooks from the top supervisors to services taking care of invoicing, it tends to be hard to control security for the sensitive highlights, for example, installments and web-based banking. To go around this, you can pick to set up various clients, giving access just to the highlights they need. Limit clients get to with the goal that each record has an exclusive set of highlights dependent on their assignments.

Online Payments through QuickBooks

Online installments through QuickBooks enables you to acknowledge installments legitimately from clients while limiting expenses. You should set up your bank subtleties, which are then utilized by clients to pay legitimately into your bank using QuickBooks. You're charged uniquely around 50 cents for every exchange, which is a lot of lower than a large number of the elective stages.

Discover the History of a Transaction

Is it accurate to say that you are burning through a huge amount of time attempting to make sense of related invoices and credit updates and installments that have been balanced against explicit invoices? To assemble more data, you should open the exchange being referred to and go to Reports>Transaction History, and you'll discover what you're searching for.

Linking Your Email to QuickBooks

In case you're selling help on the web or completing transactions that needn't bother with physical invoicing, the ideal approach to monitor transactions is to interface your email record to your QuickBooks and send your invoices directly to your client. You can also select to email reports to individuals when required. Email programs that can be connected incorporate Outlook, Gmail, and Yahoo and select others.

Viewing Double Entries

Like all bookkeeping frameworks and programming, QuickBooks additionally chips away at the rule of Double Entry. To look at the double-section of a specific transaction, you should open the transaction at that point go to Reports>Transaction Journal. This will open the Transaction Journal so you can double-check if the transaction-section is appropriately posted.

Combining Similar Accounts

Now and again, you may find that your QuickBooks scrape is hindered with various records. This happens when various employees make records for various assignments or when numerous client accounts have been wrongly made. To make your last records simpler, mixing is the best choice. This should be possible by picking one record name, at that point, setting off to another record for mixing. Right-click and then paste and the name of the record you need all to be converted to. At the point when you click Save, QuickBooks will inquire as to whether you need to combine the records. Snap-on, Yes.

Chat with Staff

QuickBooks offers staff with various records an opportunity to visit through the QuickBooks window, which empowers your group to sort out the issues or examine passages into the framework. To talk, open up Company>Chat with a Coworker and start another visit.

Offset Invoices against Credit Notes

One of the significant focuses which can make QuickBooks a problem to utilize is that invoices vanish from the record if they're balanced to zero against credit notes. To avoid this, circulate credit notes against various invoices, so only one receipt doesn't vanish.

Printing Batch Invoices

If you need to print numerous invoices one after another, the best thing is to pick Batch Printing. Here, you should make your invoices, click on the bolt beside Print, and snap-on Print Batch. This will give you an alternative to pick receipt numbers for printing, which makes it simpler for you.

Let's Be Clear About What QuickBooks Online Advanced is Not

Need Care, and the Customer Success Manager gave by QuickBooks Online Advanced are not ProAdvisors® and don't offer similar services bookkeeping proficient does. Their job is to free you up from investigating issues so you can concentrate your time on the things that issue most to you and your customers. They additionally fill in as a single purpose of contact at Intuit® for any product that gives your customers experience overall contributions. They can even prescribe training from a rundown of self-managed alternatives that might bear some significance with your customers and answer any inquiries you or your customers may have about Intuit programming you're thinking about.

QuickBooks Online Advanced isn't Available on Wholesale… Yet

We realize that our bookkeeping experts esteem the capacity to pay for their customers' product through one bound together with the bill and welcome the association we show by offering an exclusive discount. We will update you as often as possible on our arrangements for a discount rebate as they create.

QuickBooks Online Advanced Will Continue to Evolve and isn't done yet

This is the initial move toward an adaptation of QuickBooks Online that fathoms the necessities of clients who are exceeding QuickBooks Online Plus – and your input will assist us with making it more grounded.

You Can Shape QuickBooks Online Advanced

This month, we are imparting the new offering to a little gathering of QuickBooks Online Plus clients. You are best situated to decide whether QuickBooks Online Advanced is directly for your customers. We urge you to have discussions with them about it, and we strive to give you the data you have to reinforce your situation as their most trusted in counsel.

Help and Support:

In-item support

To get to online assistance;

1. Select the question mark symbol in the upper right corner of the QuickBooks Online screen.

2. Type in your question in the search box to find a solution.

3. To refine the question, you can click Refine and drop-down choice criteria, for this situation, Product.

4. When you have found the important article, click on the going to dispatch it.

QB Assistant

Advanced assistants are changing how we use services, and now iPhones Siri has some challenges. On the off chance that you are searching for assists like With googling Home (OK Google), Amazon Alexa, or comparable, you will be happy to realize that QuickBooks Online has launched our QB Assistant.

QB Assistant is in beta right now yet is functional and ready to help.

To turn QB Assistant on;

1. Login to your QuickBooks Online record.

2. Click on the gear symbol and select QuickBooks Labs from the Settings list.

3. Look to find the alternative QB Assistant and snap on the slider on the privilege to guarantee it is in the 'ON' position.

4. Click done in the base right-hand corner of the screen

To utilize QB Assistant;

To begin your dialogue with QB in QuickBooks Online using the work area program, click the symbol in the upper right corner in the middle of the Help and Gear symbols there are some pre-populated questions you can tap on, any way you can type into the questions box.

Conclusion

QuickBooks can enable an organization to run all the more easily and viably. It keeps data composed helpfully. Seeing how the product functions are basic for QuickBooks to be utilized in the proposed manner. Since you have finished this instructional exercise, you ought to be prepared to begin investigating more. Try not to let your insight into QuickBooks end here. Find out about the further developed highlights of QuickBooks and modify it to turn into your product.

www.ingramcontent.com/pod-product-compliance
Lightning Source LLC
Chambersburg PA
CBHW070630220526
45466CB00001B/141